CREATIVE Chaos

CREATIVE Chaos

PAIGE DOWDING

iUniverse®

CREATIVE CHAOS

iUniverse books may be ordered through booksellers or by contacting:

iUniverse
1663 Liberty Drive
Bloomington, IN 47403
www.iuniverse.com
844-349-9409

ISBN: 978-1-6632-3658-6 (sc)
ISBN: 978-1-6632-3659-3 (e)

Print information available on the last page.

iUniverse rev. date: 02/28/2022

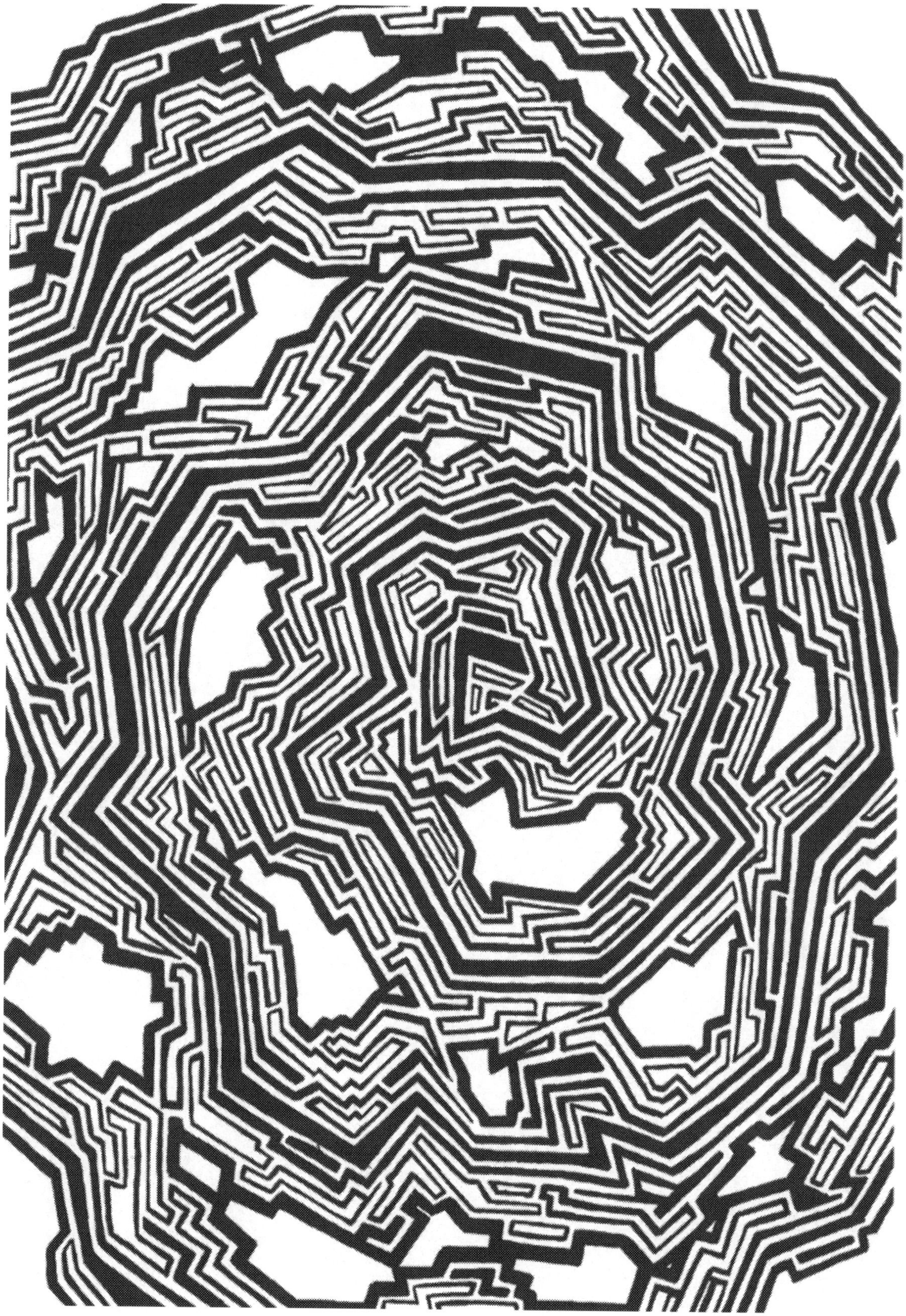

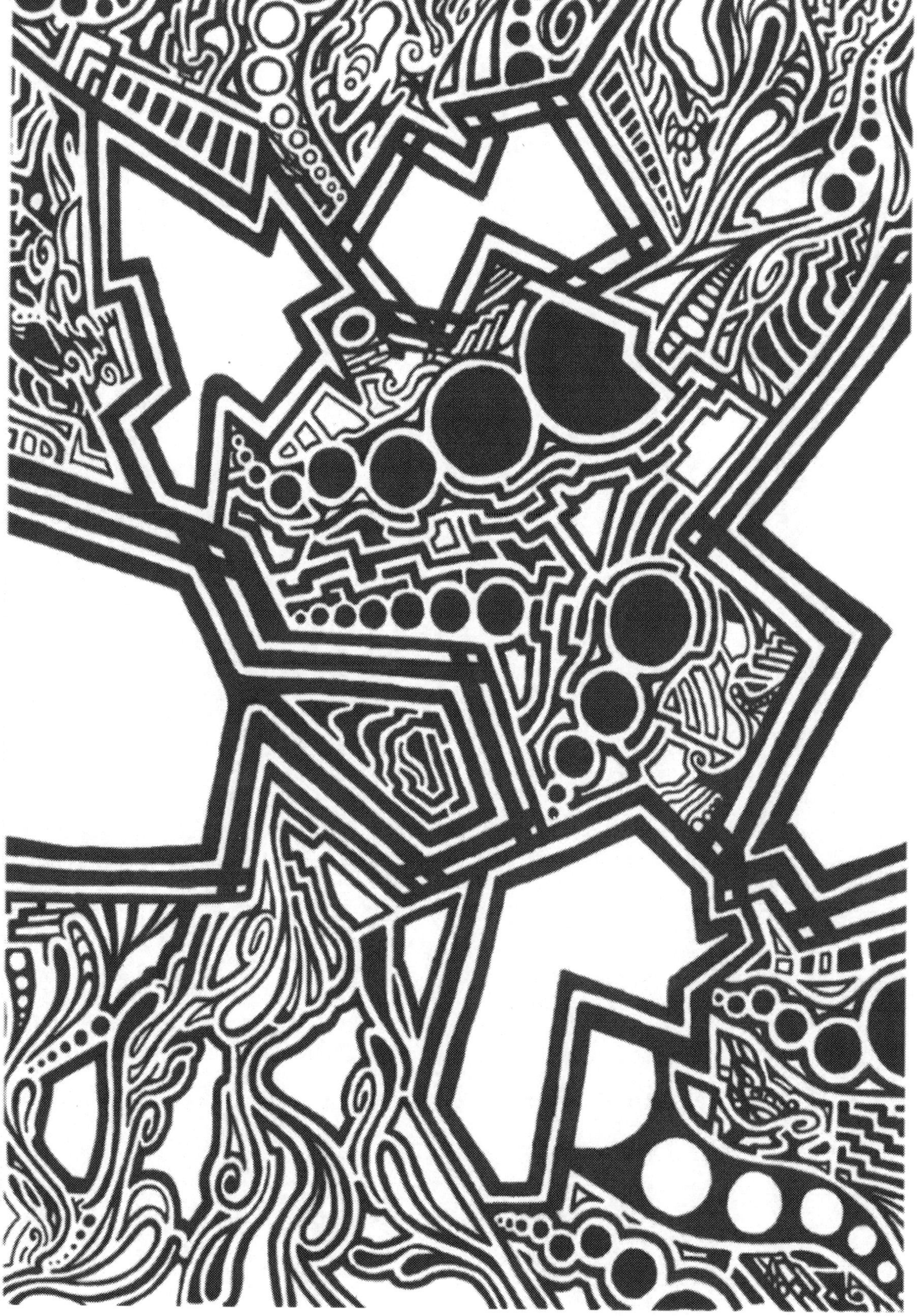

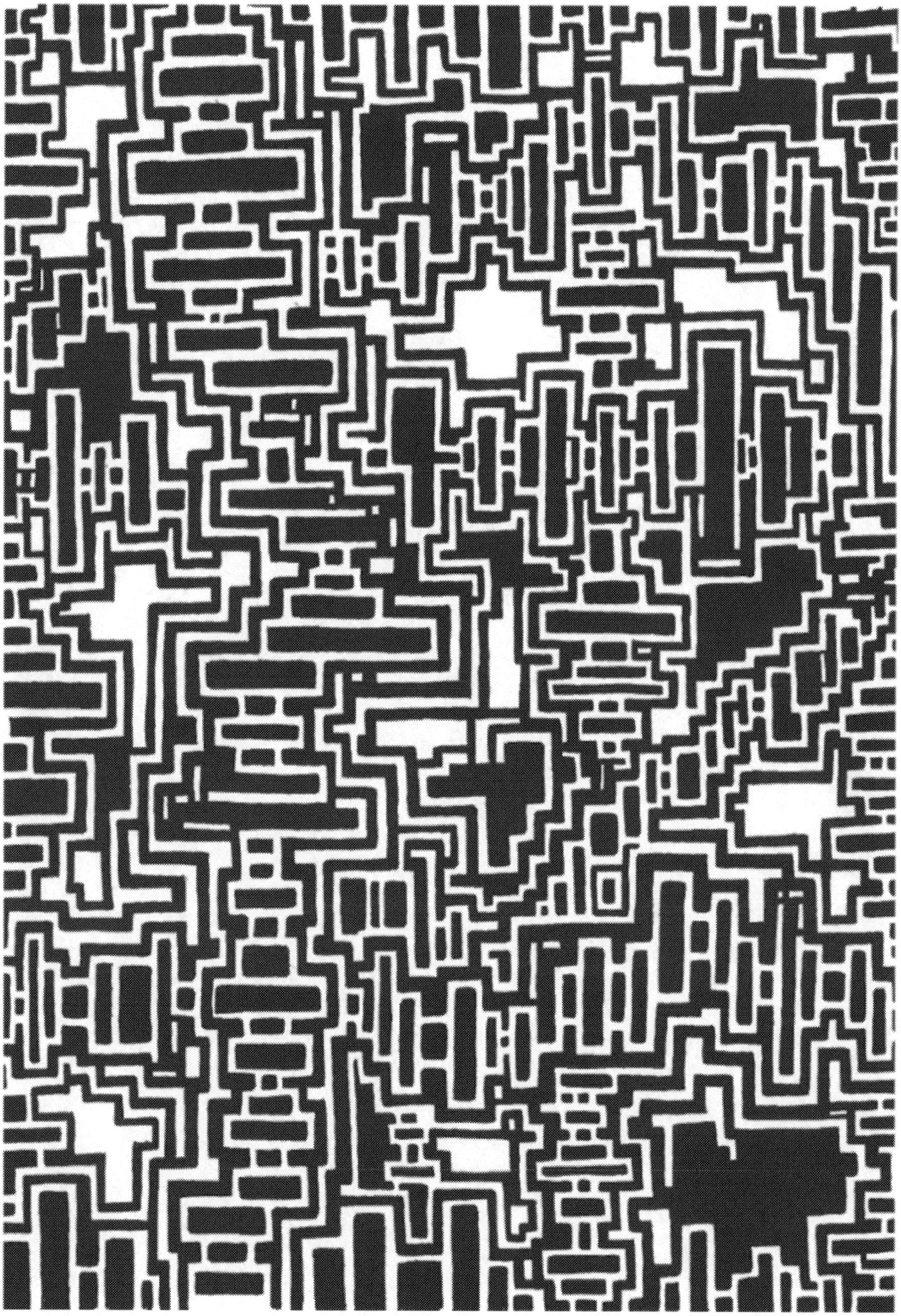

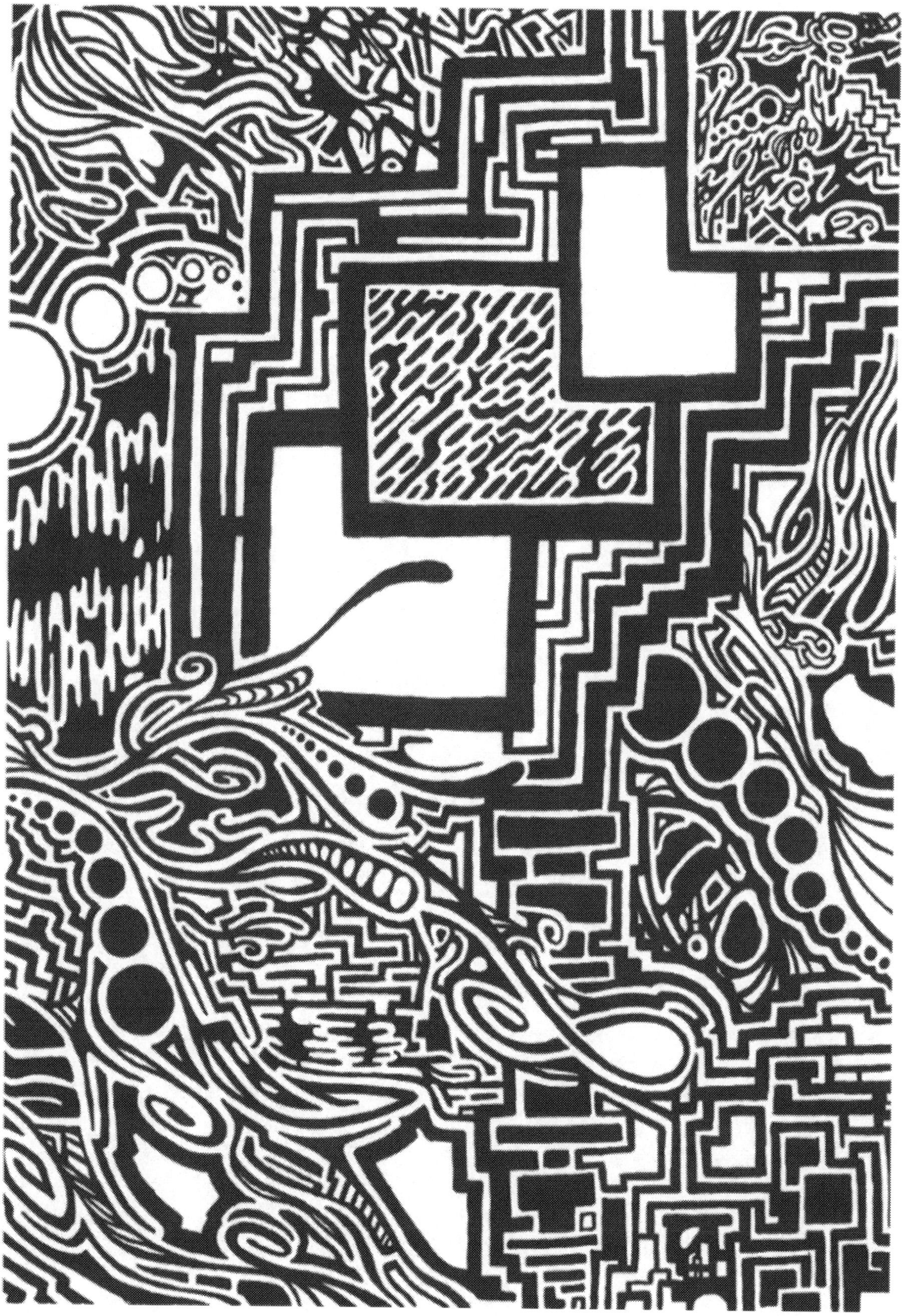

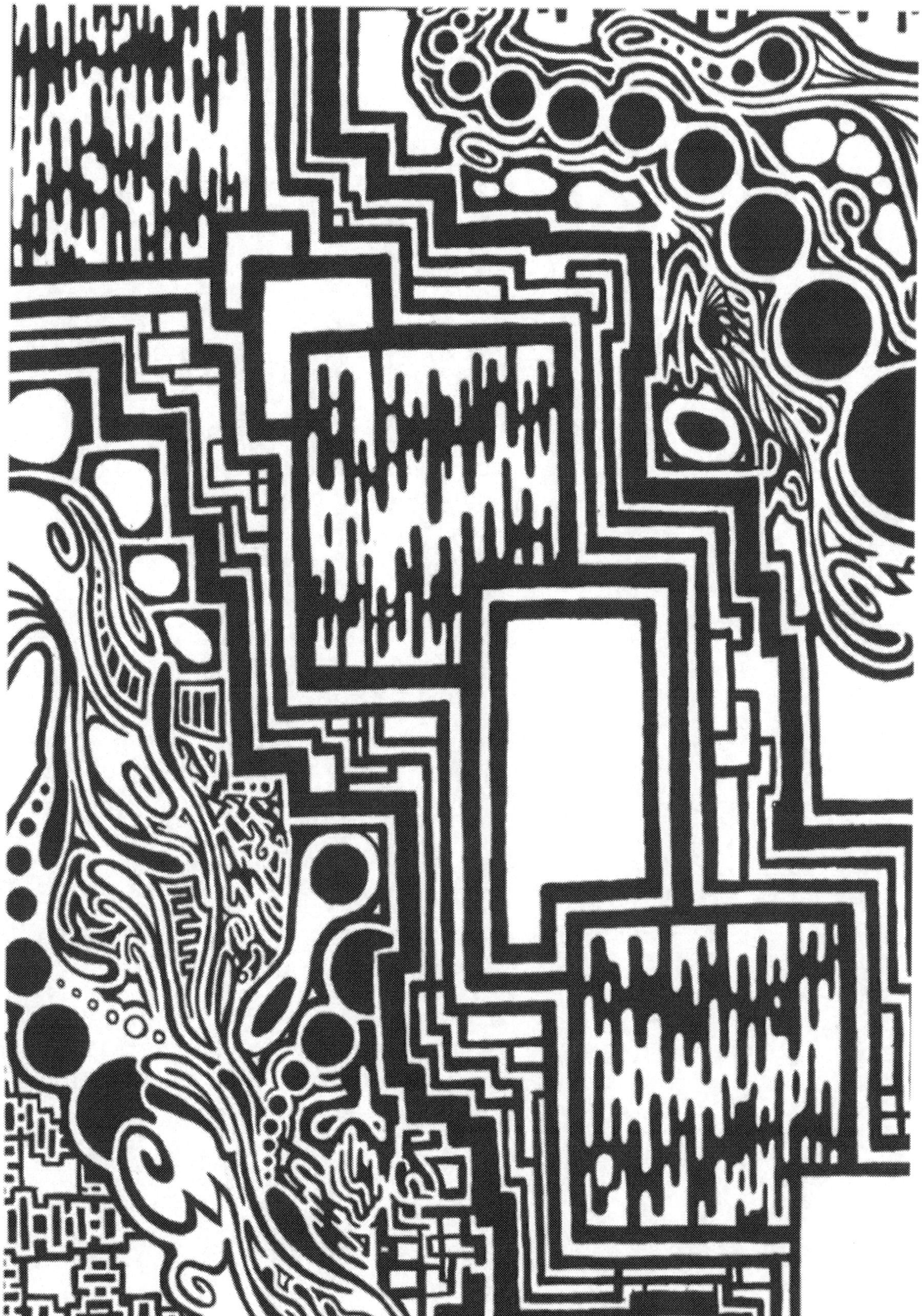

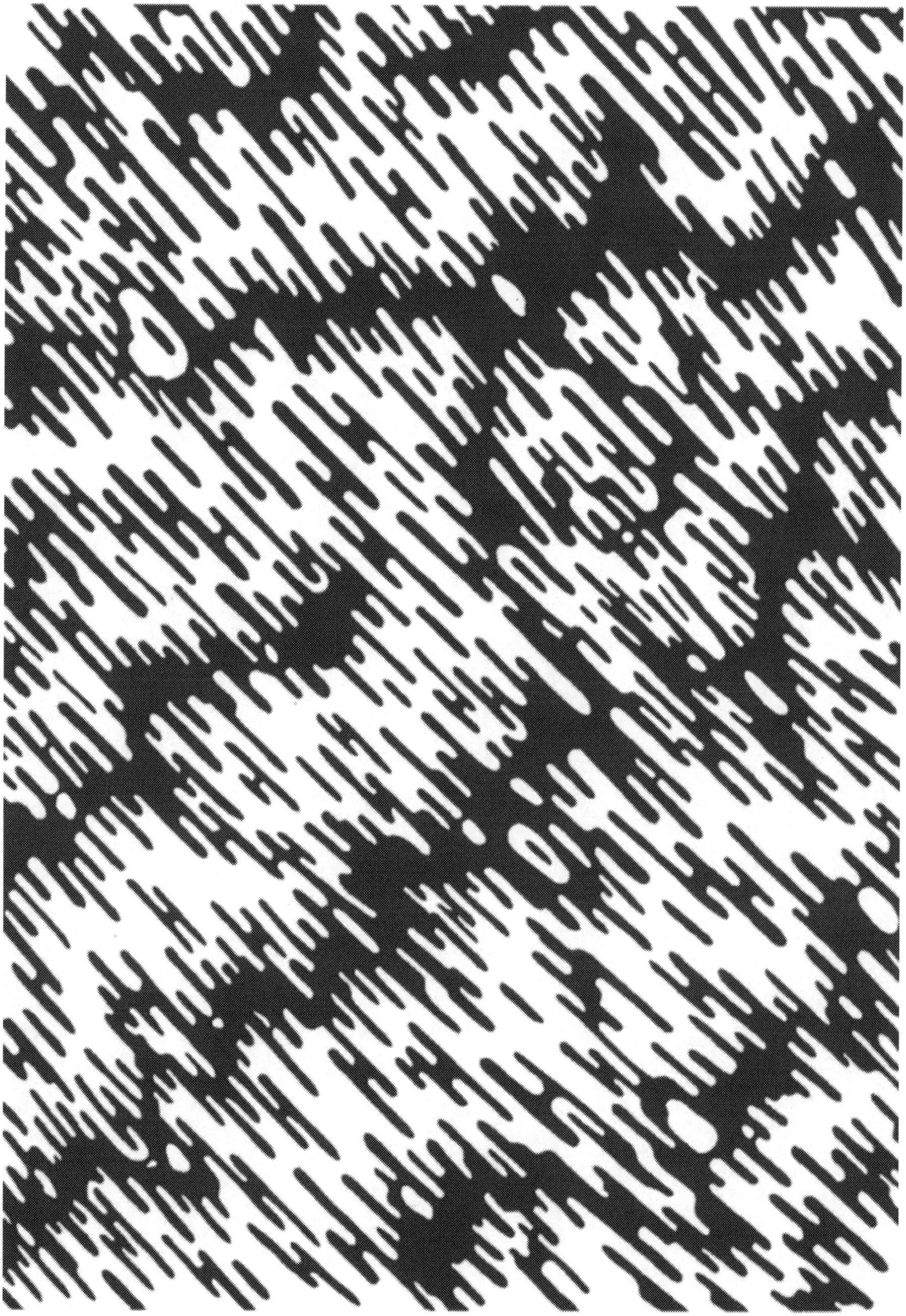

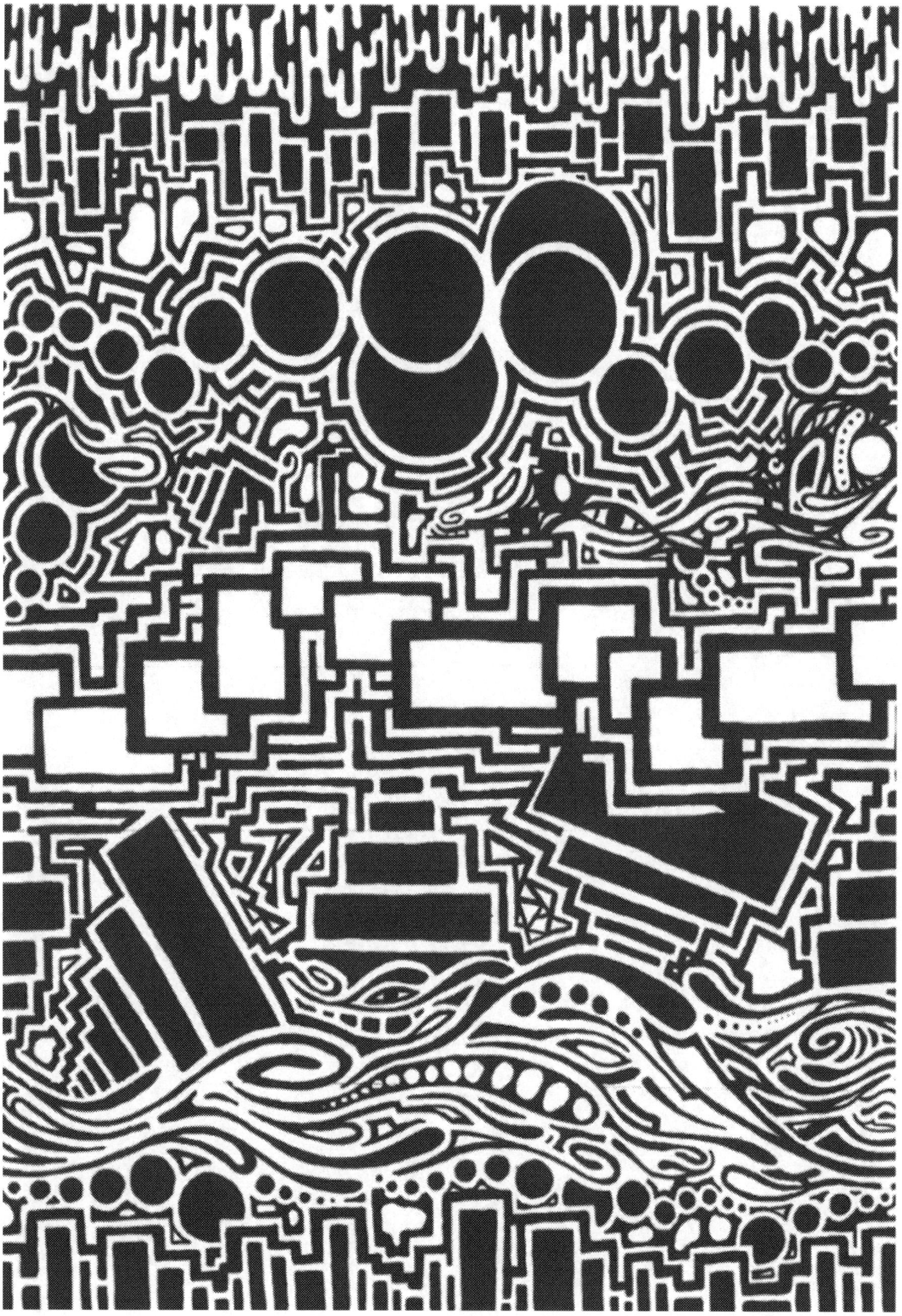

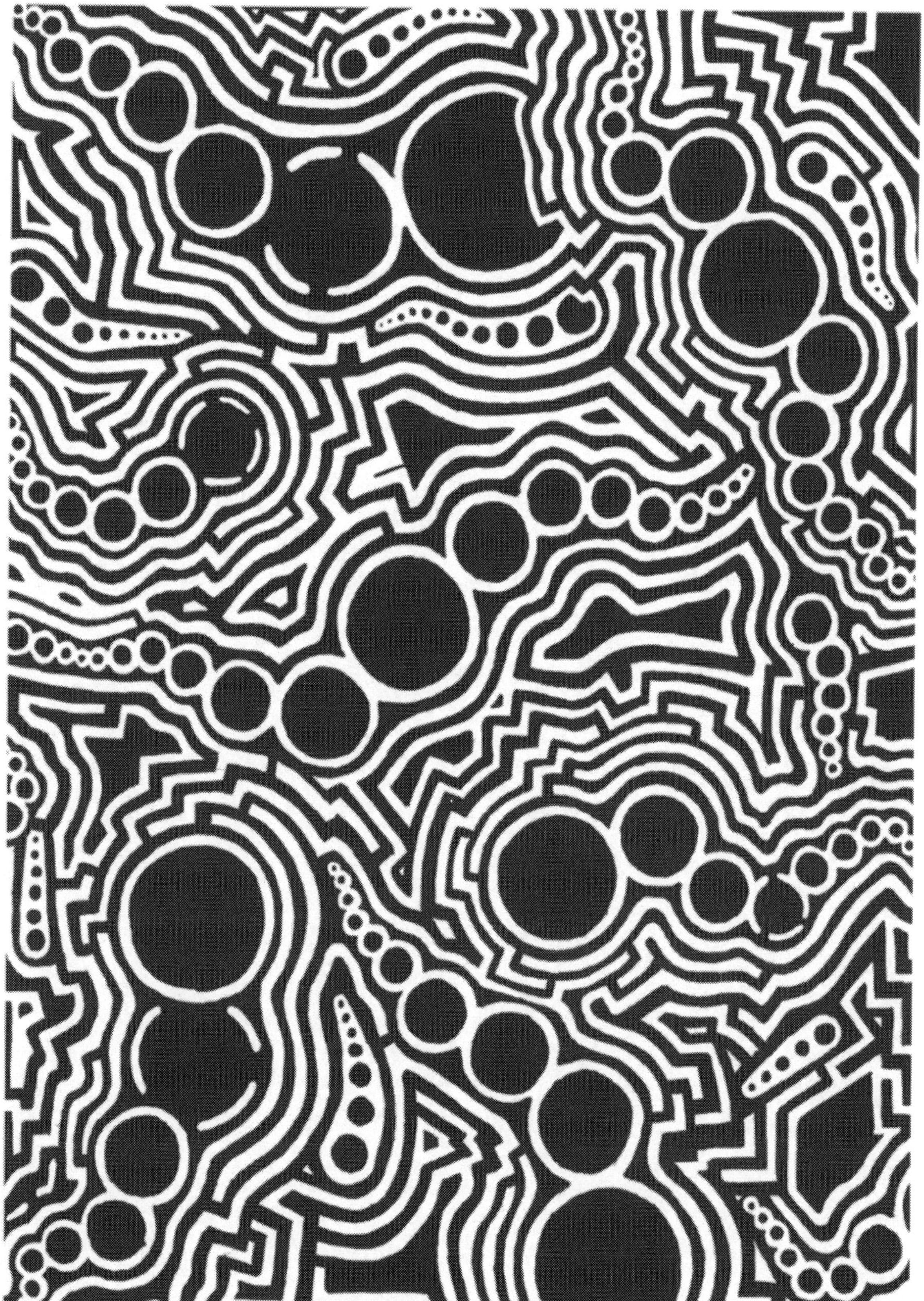

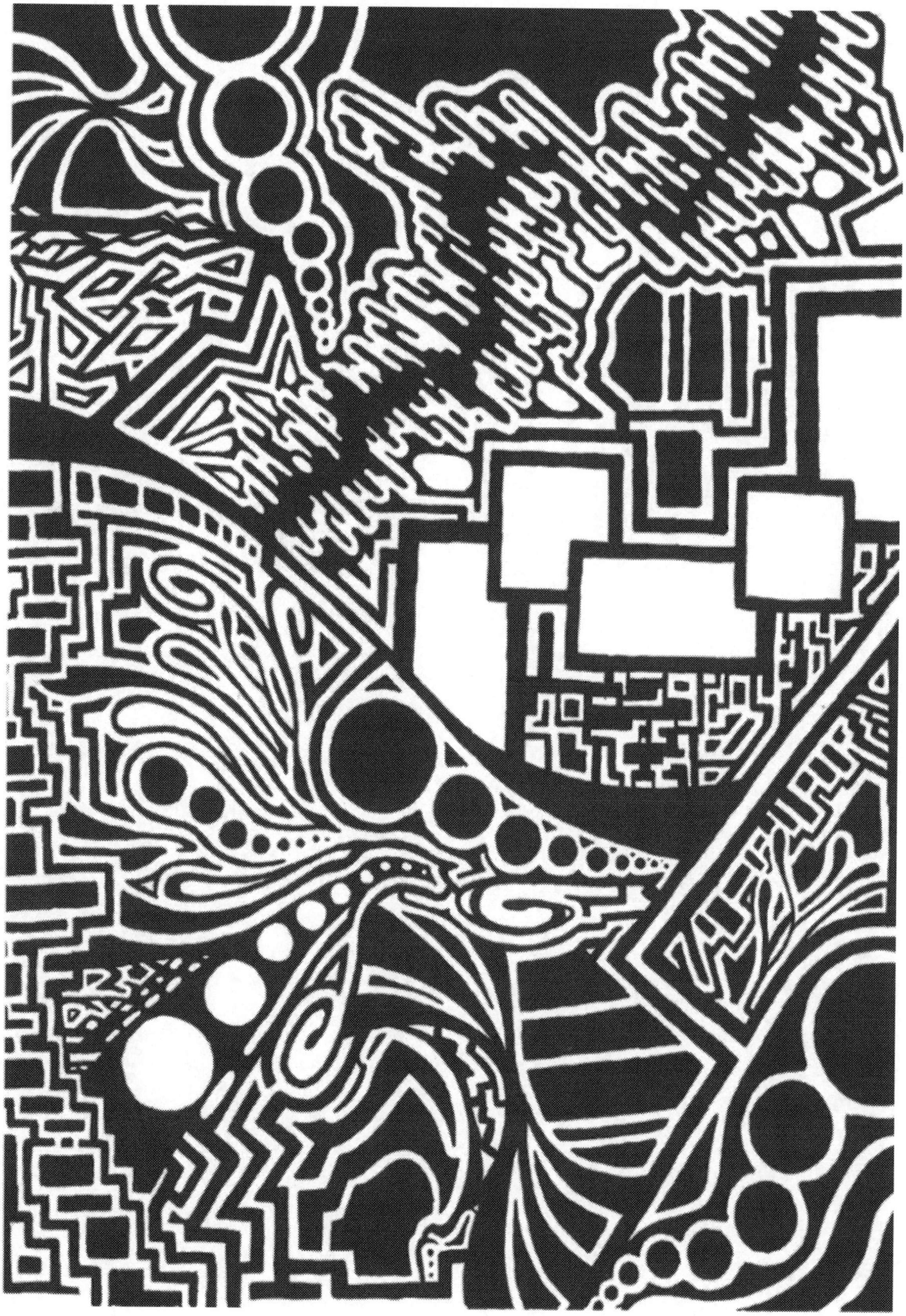

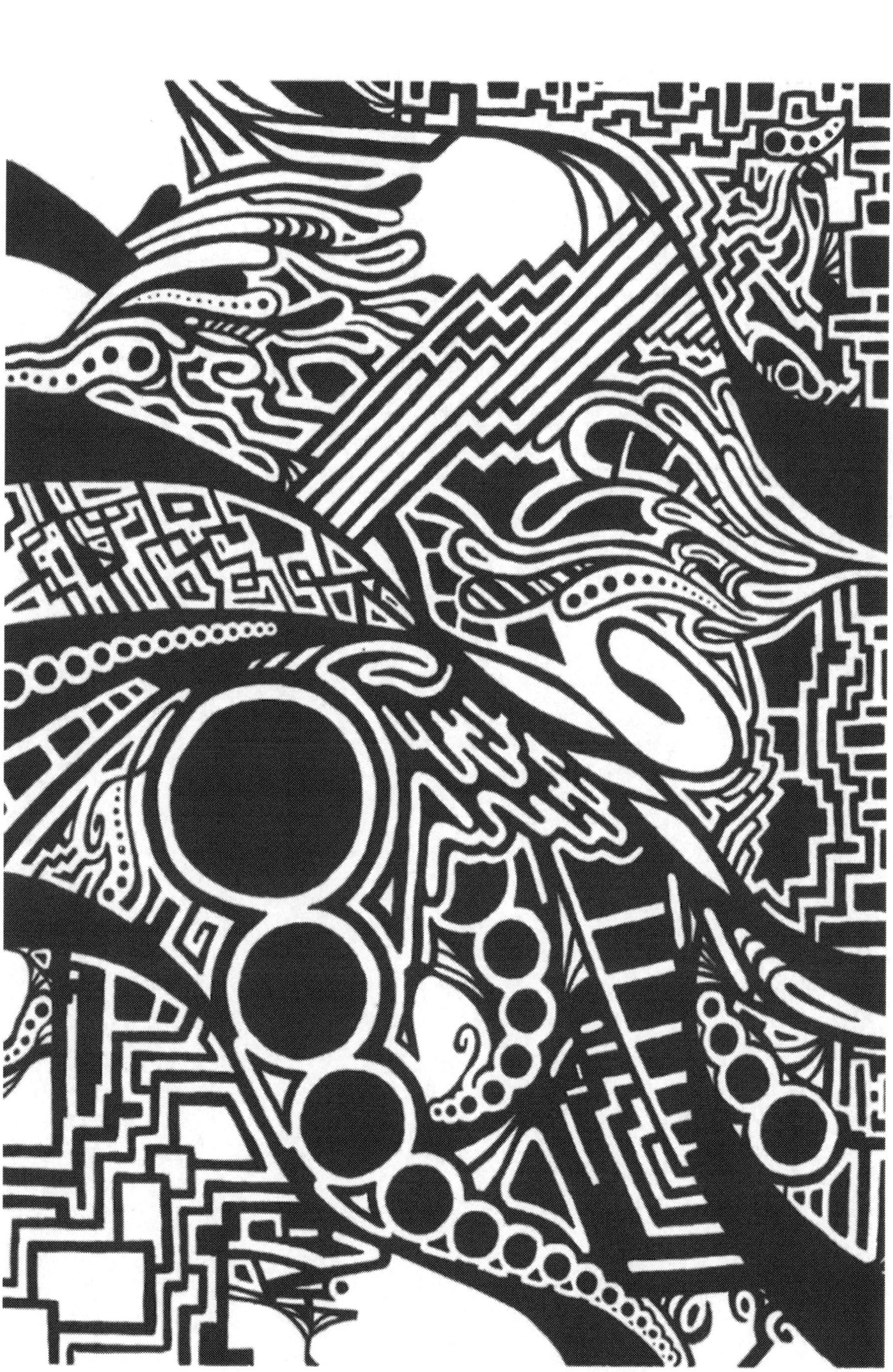

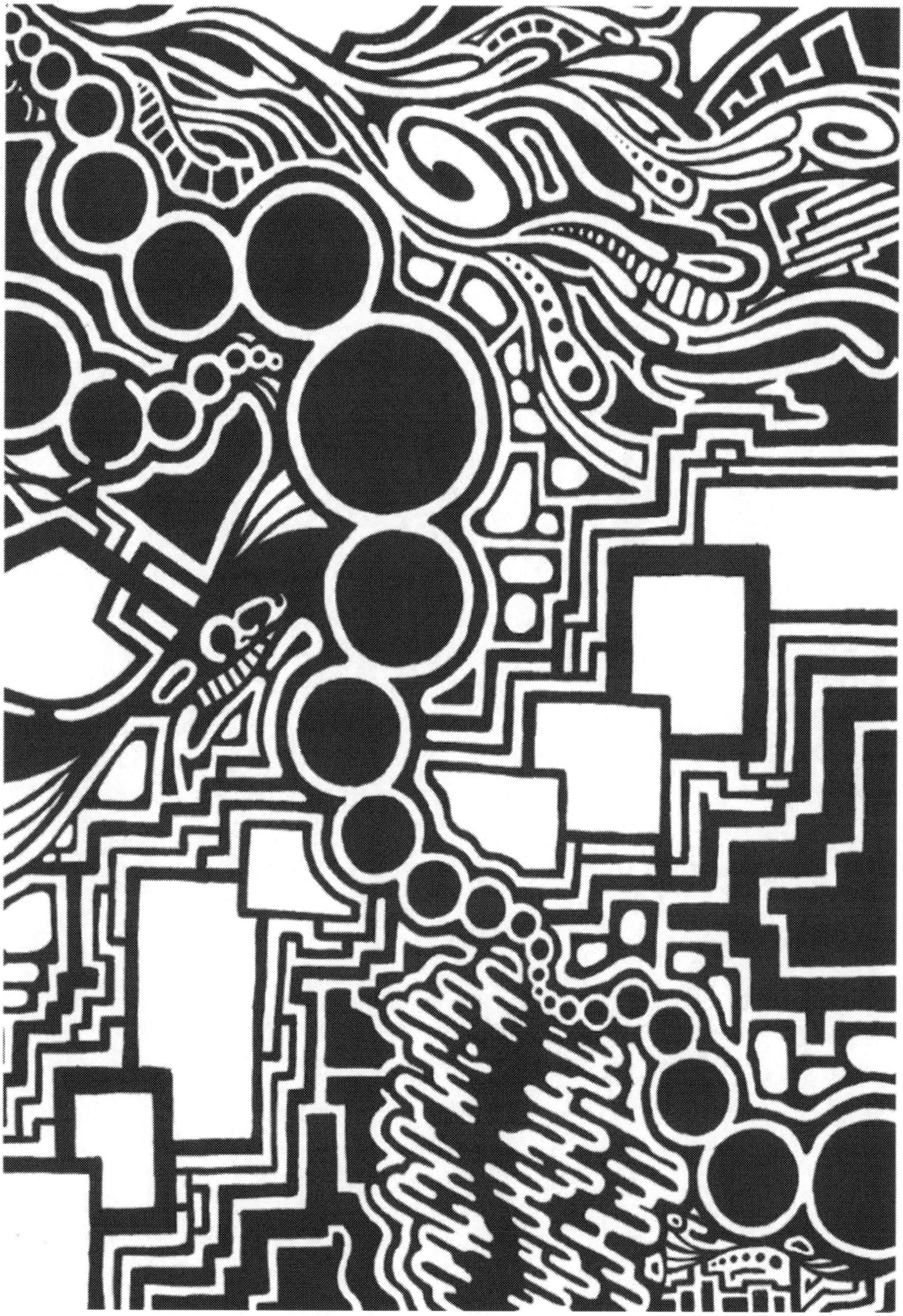

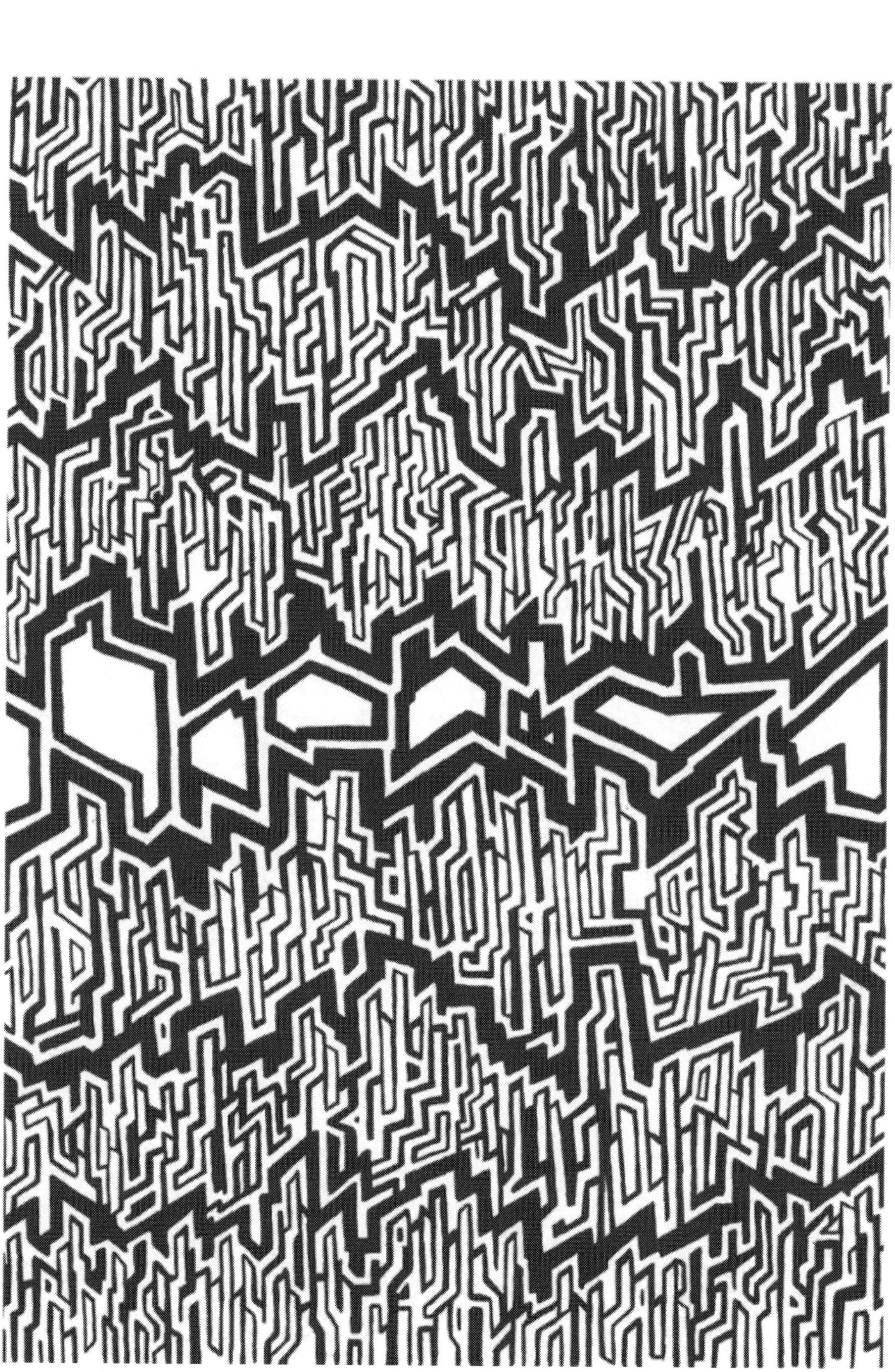

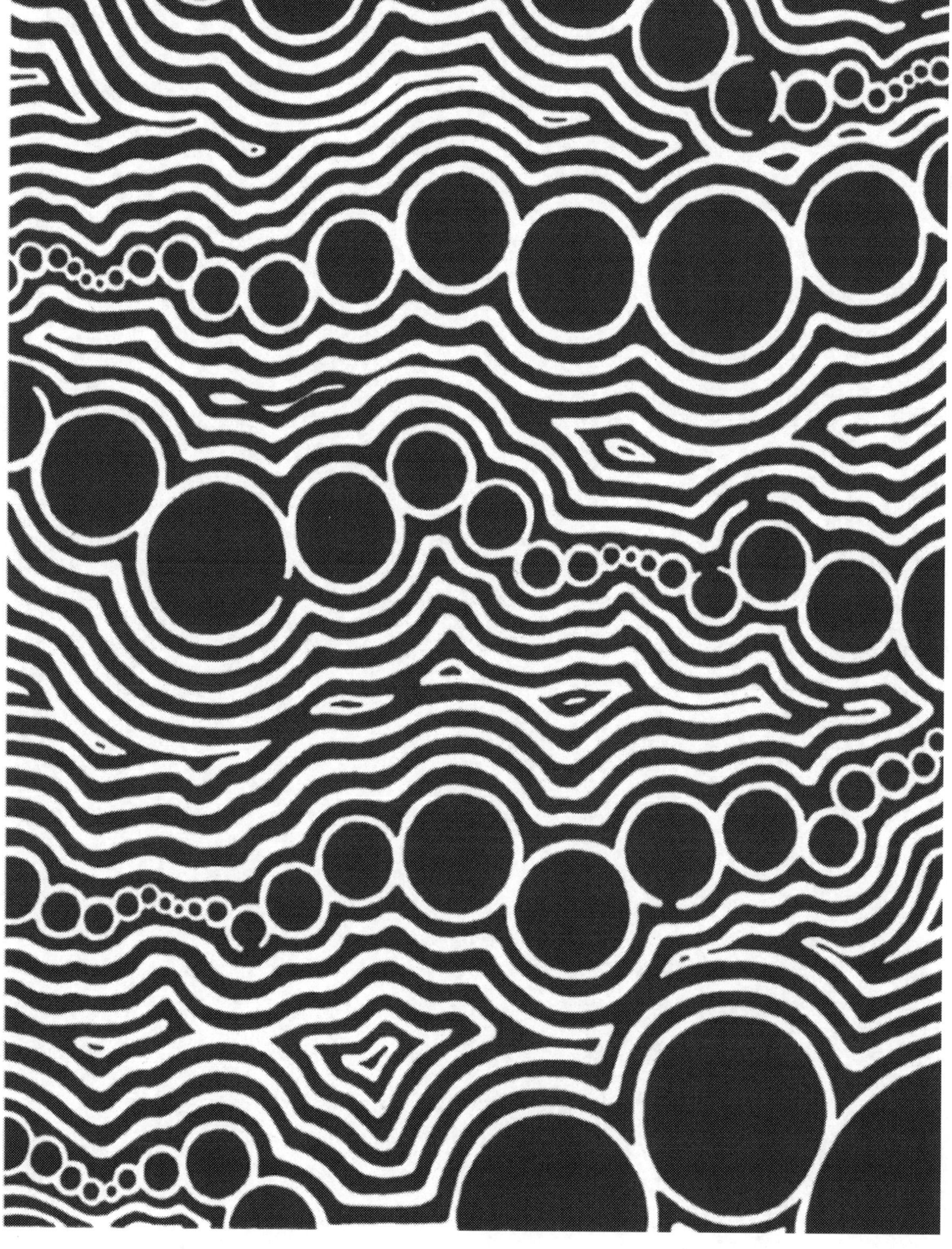

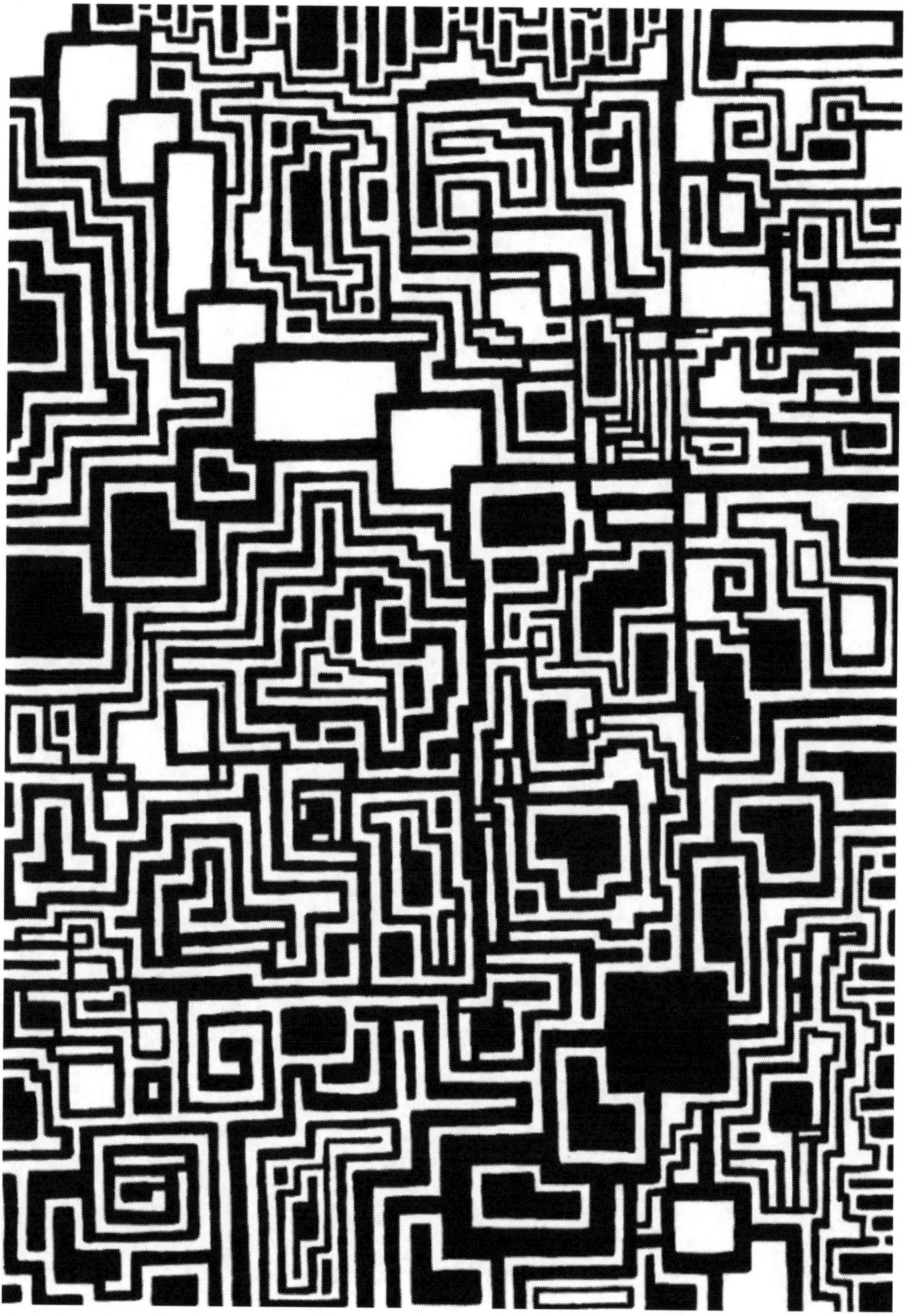

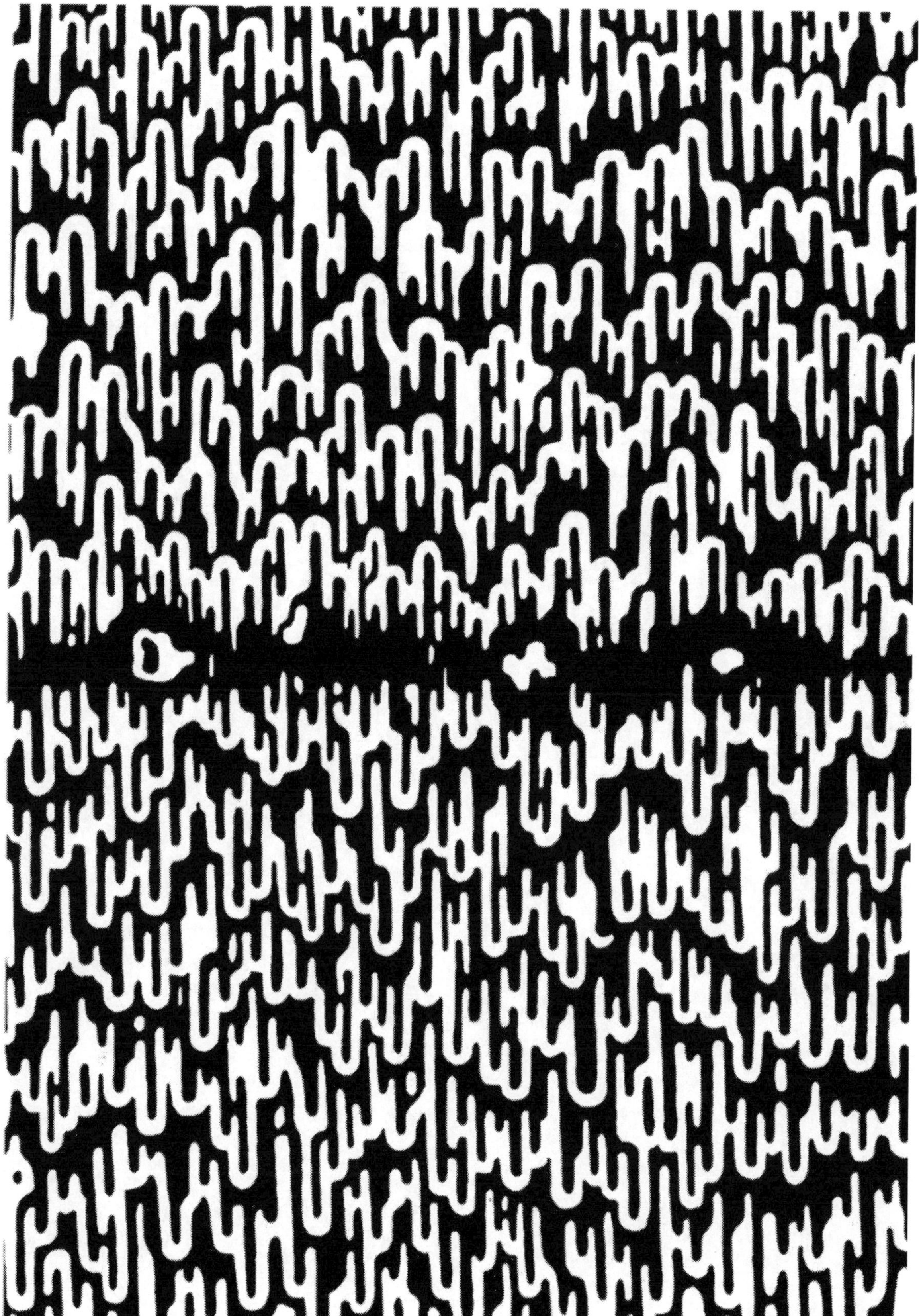

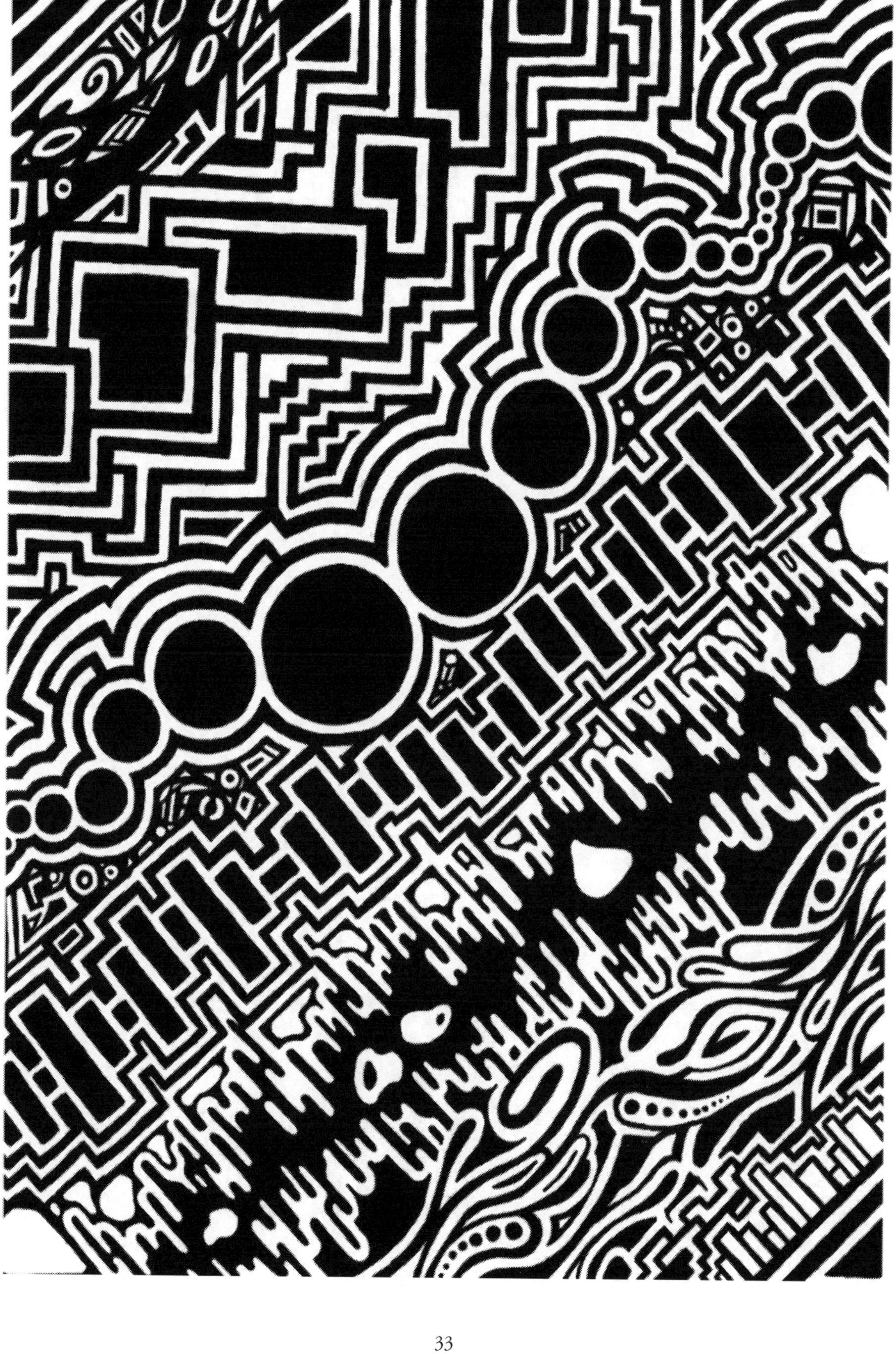

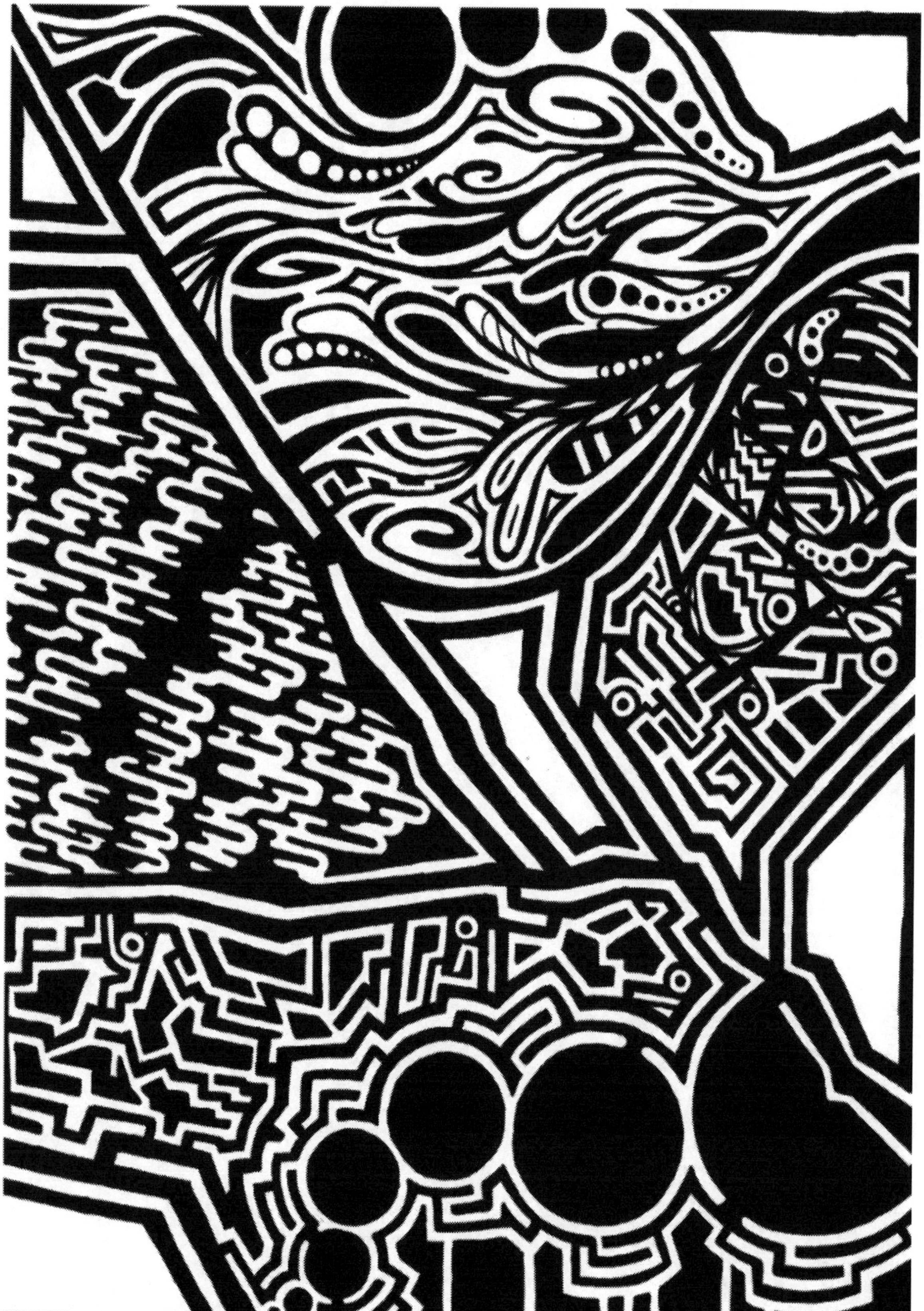

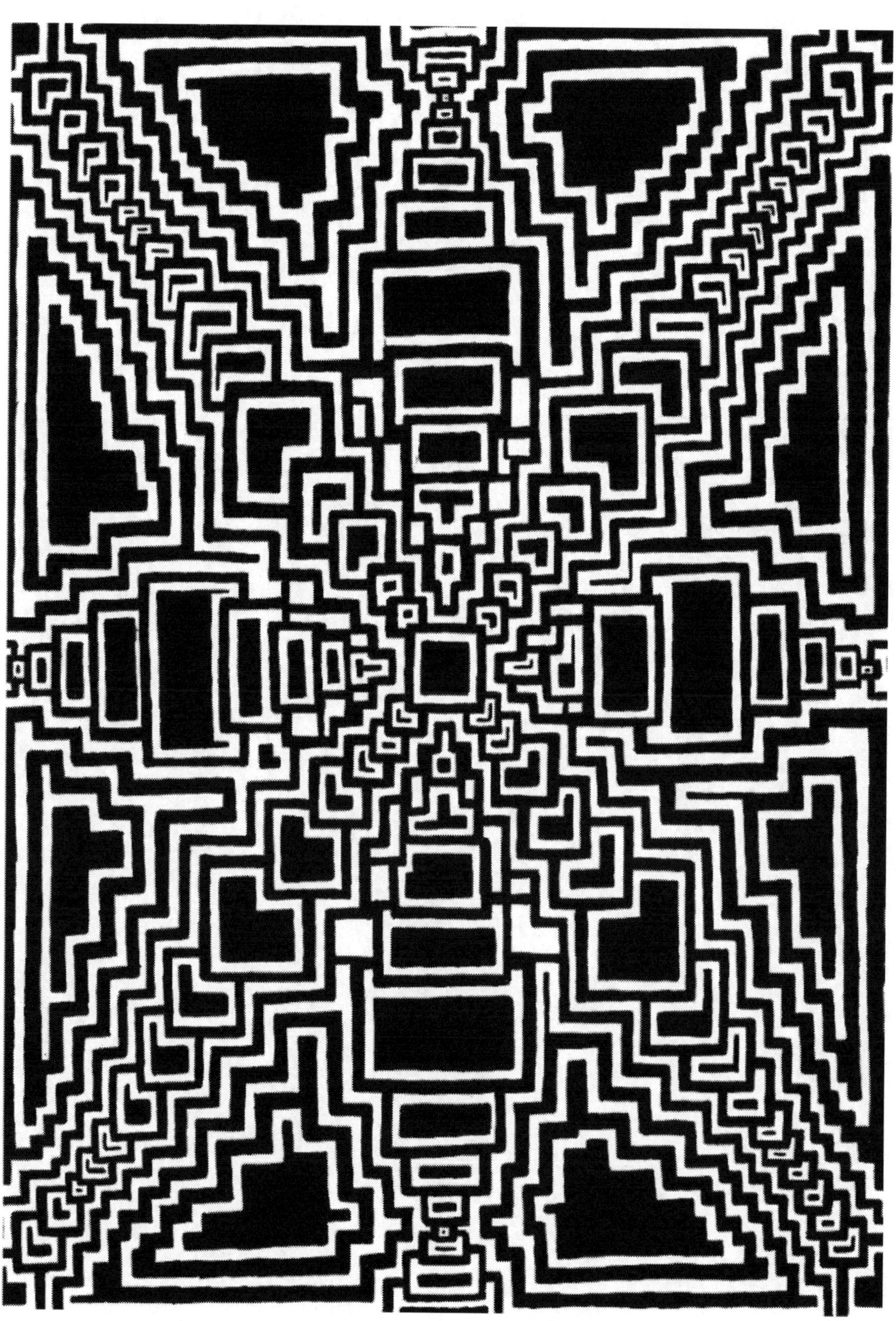

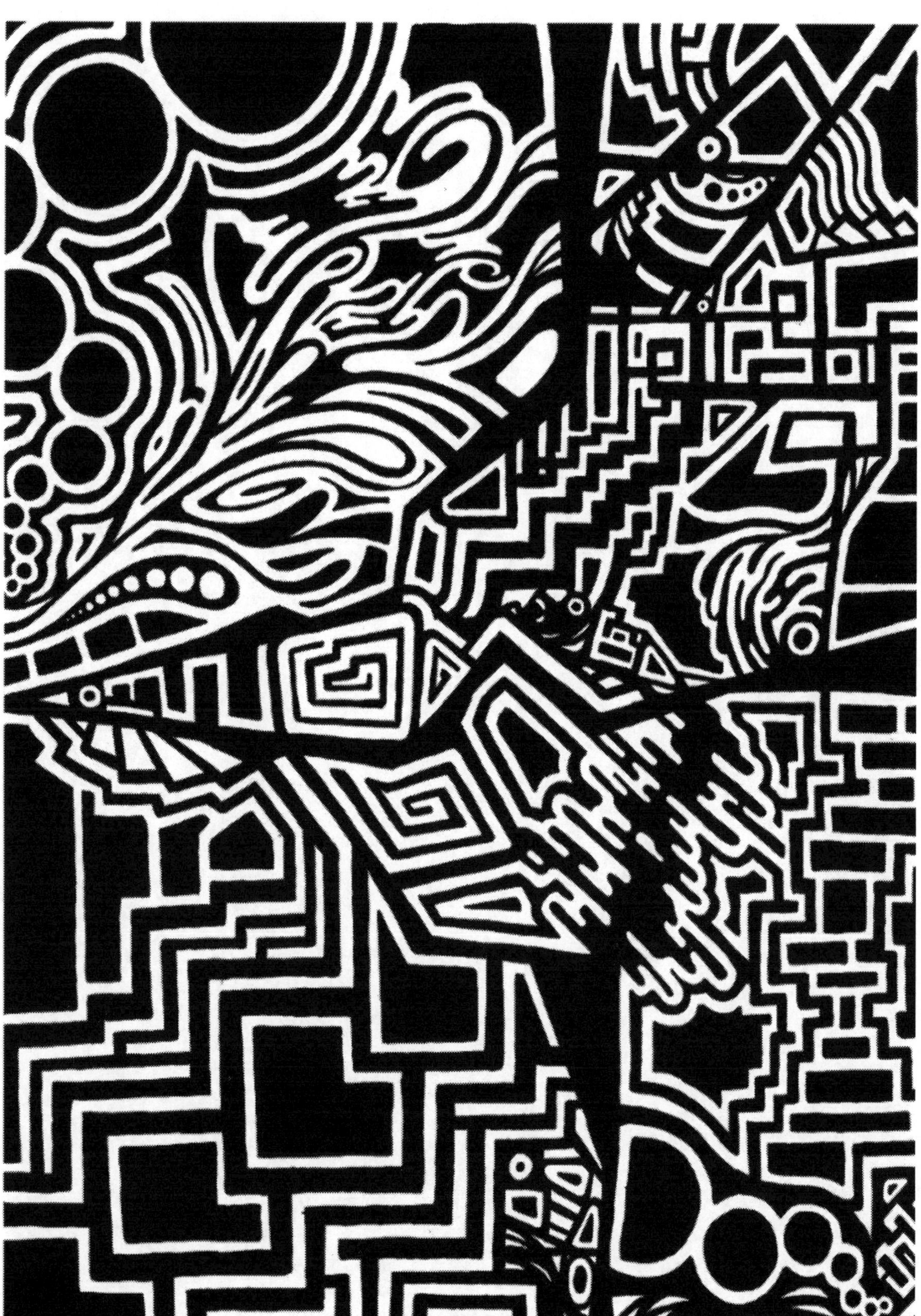

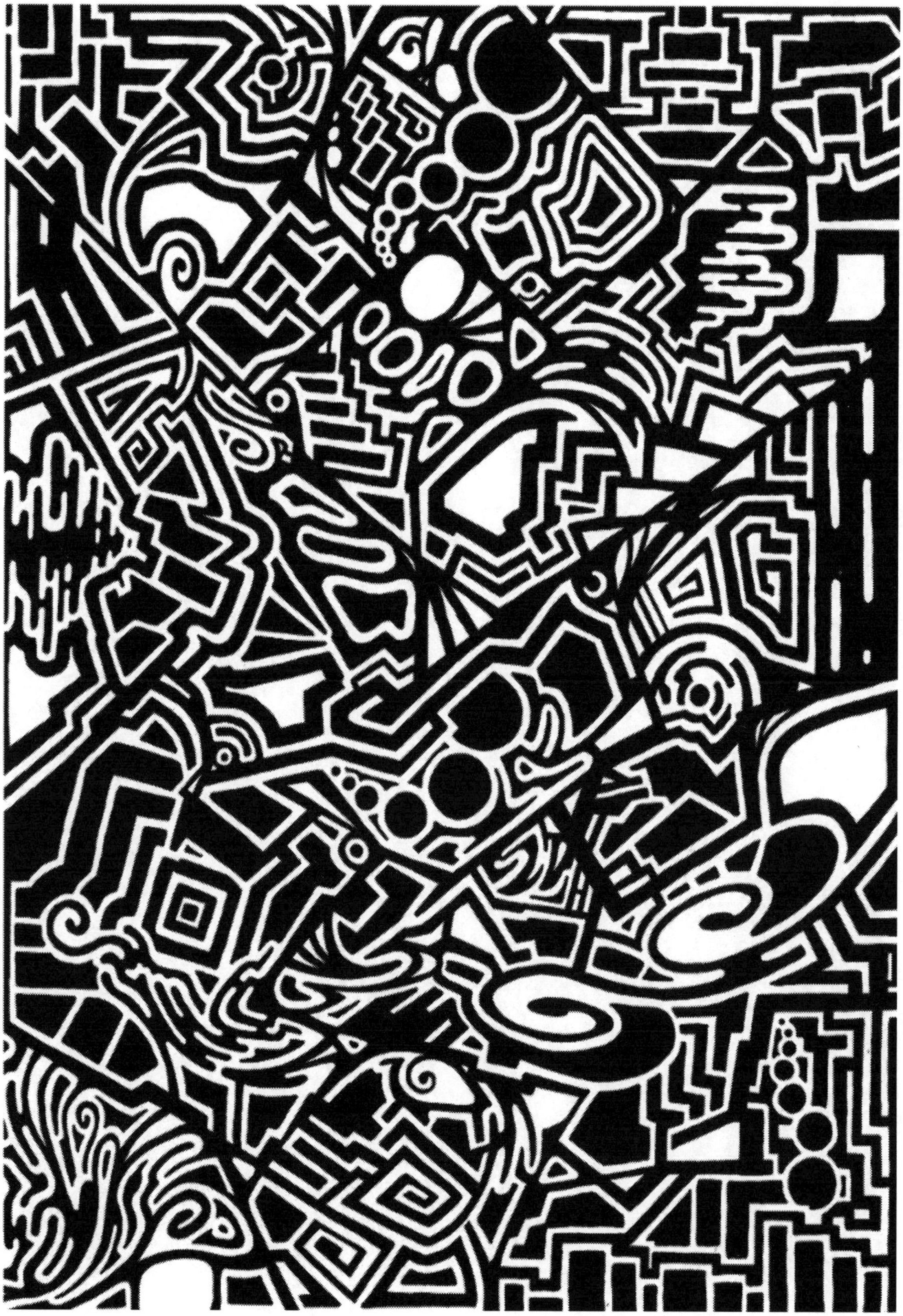

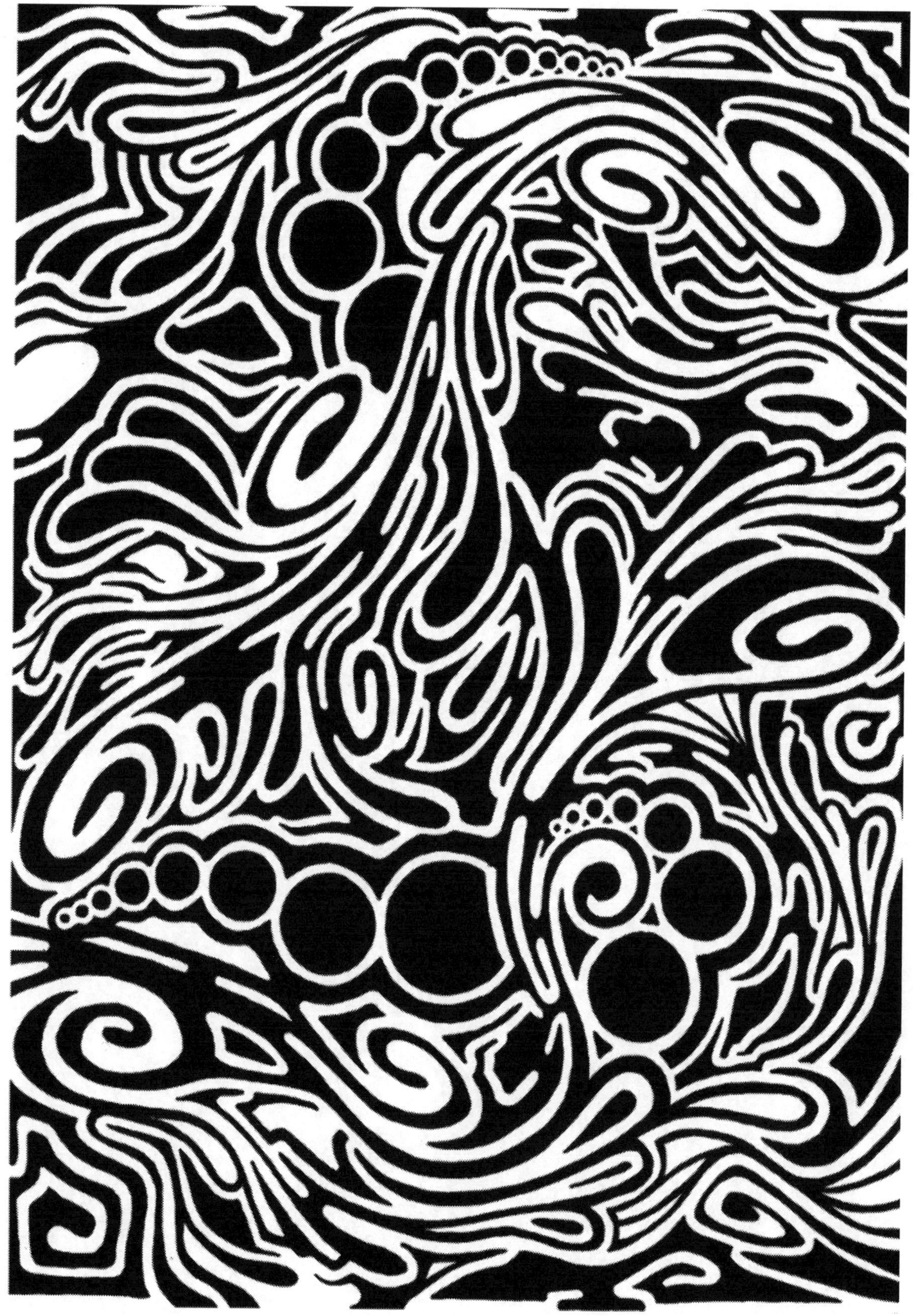

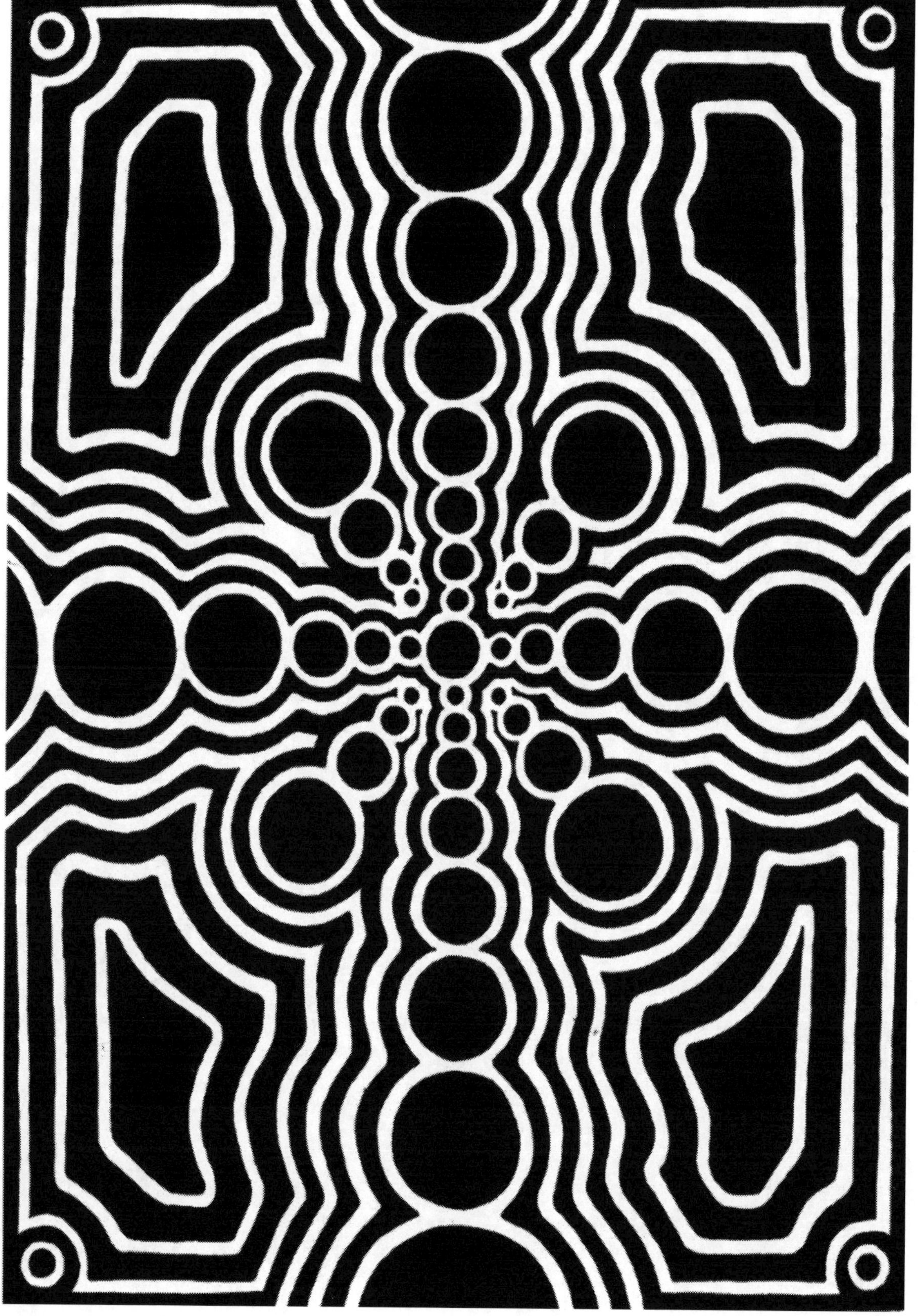

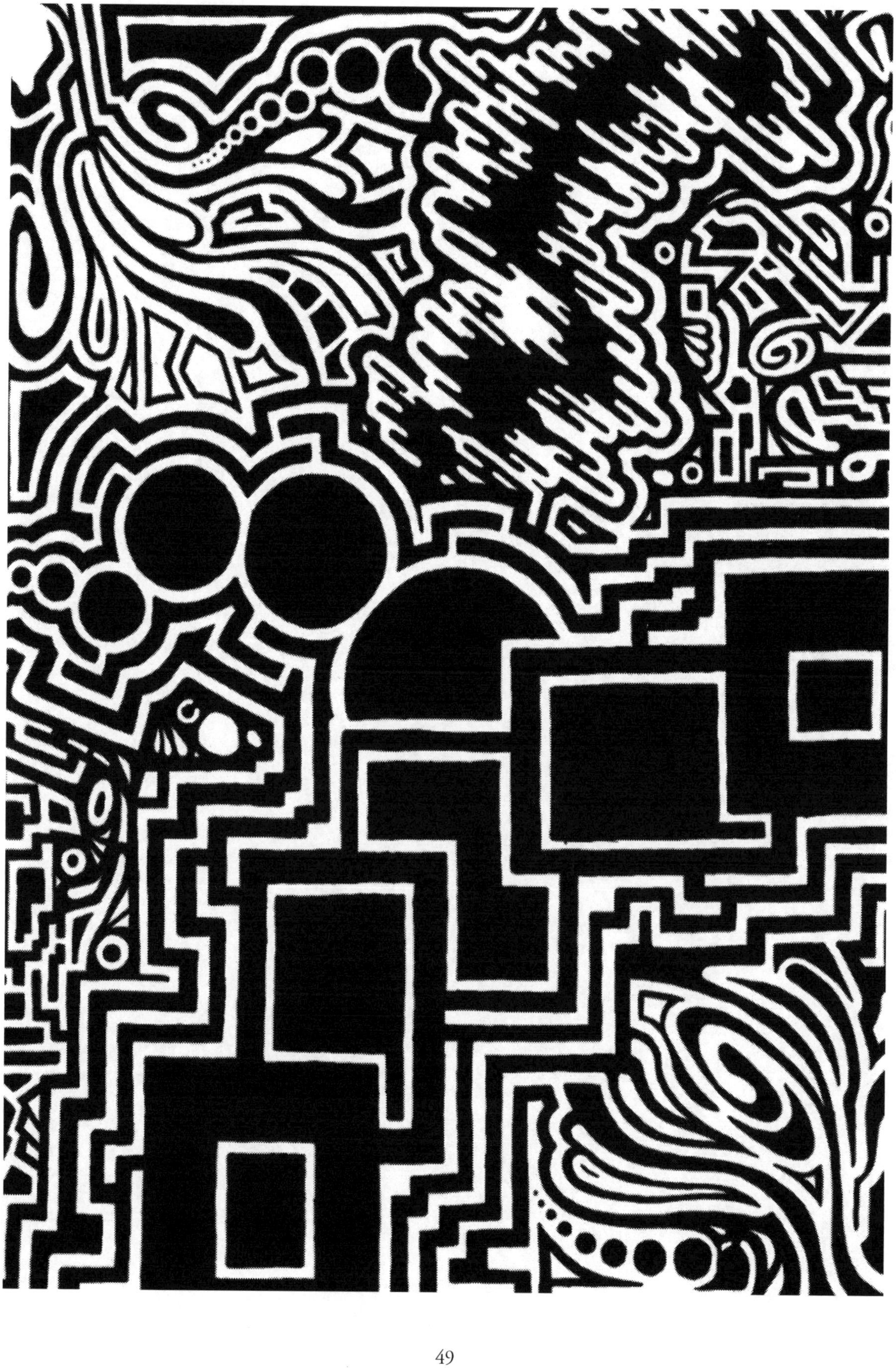

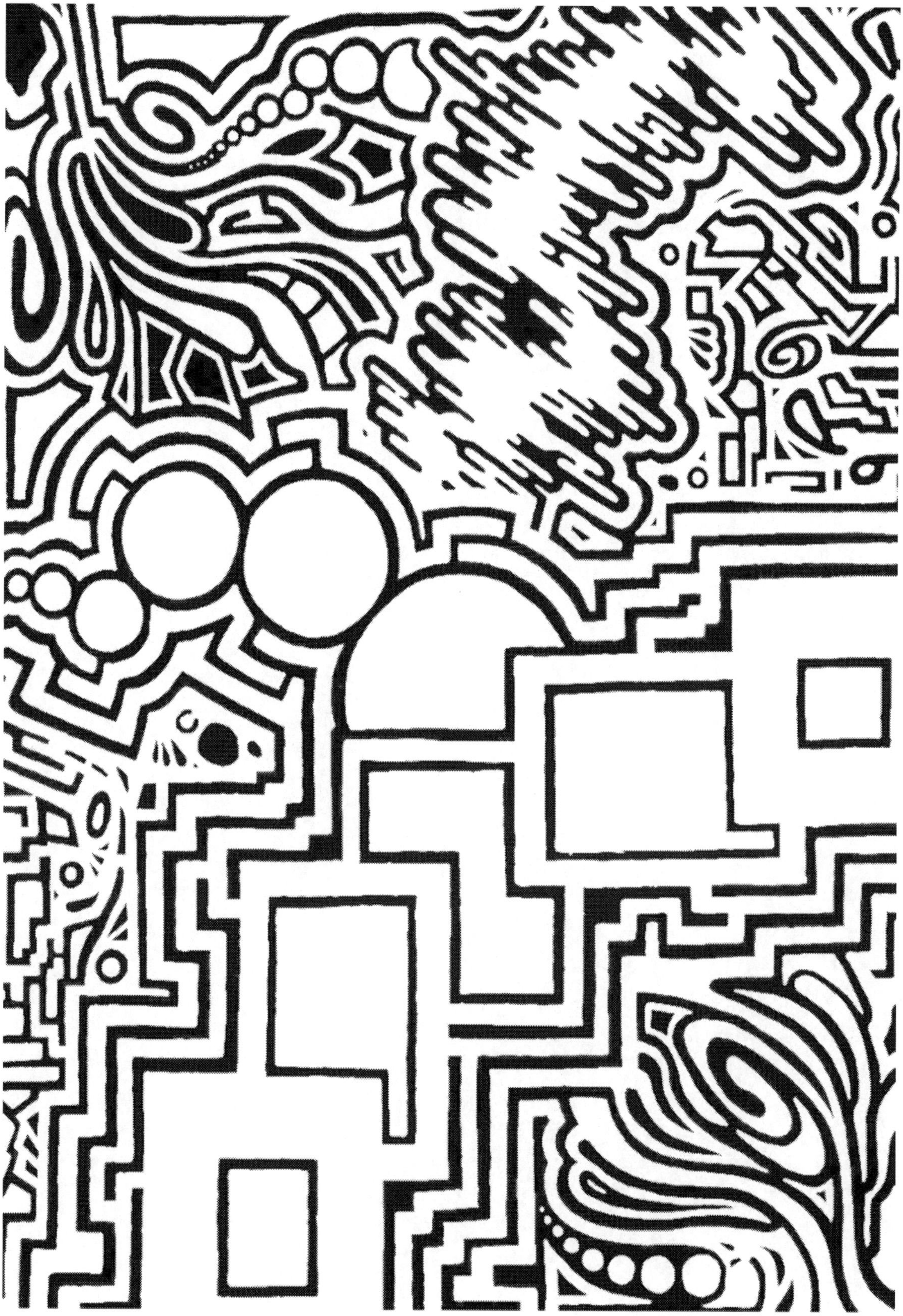

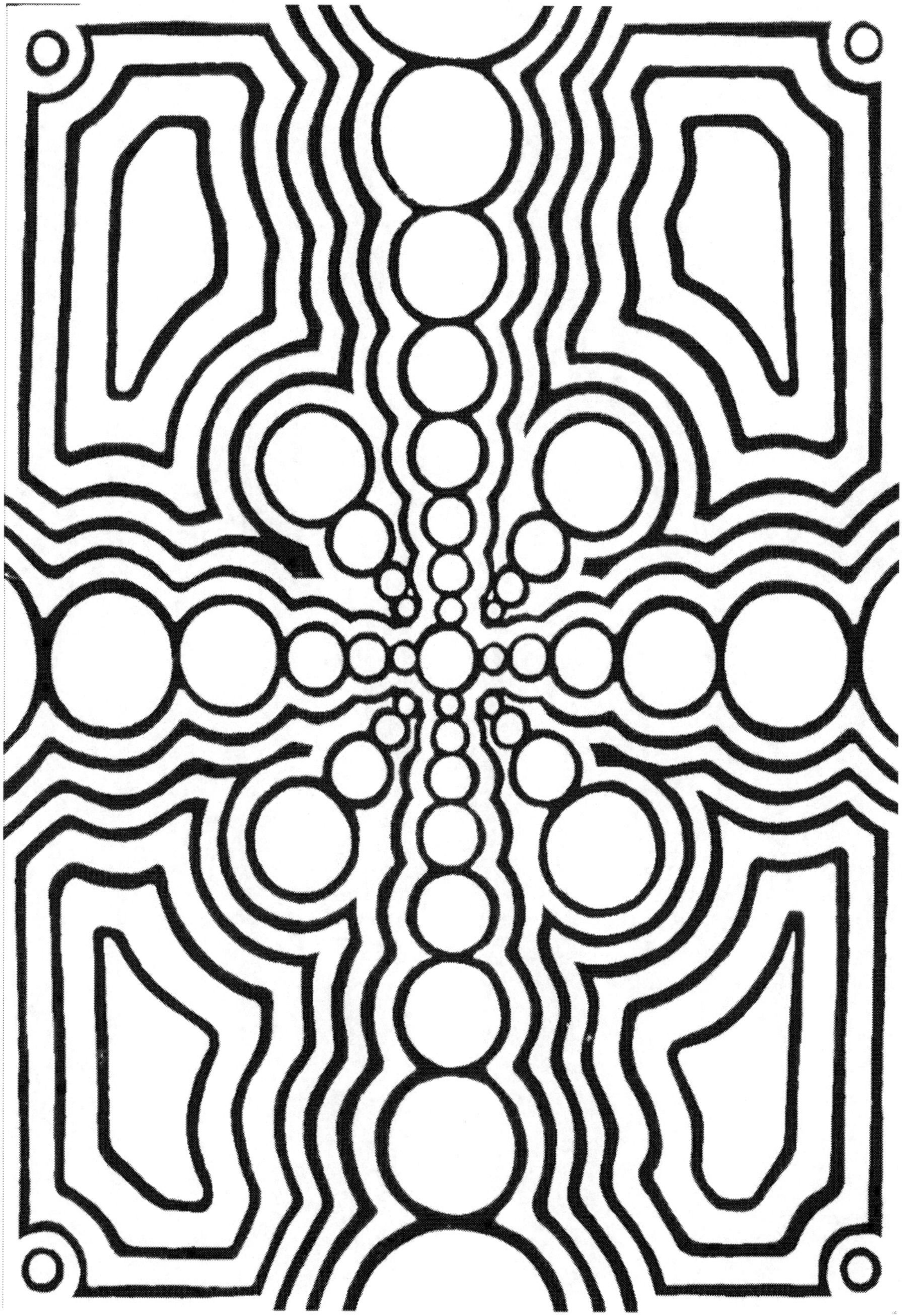

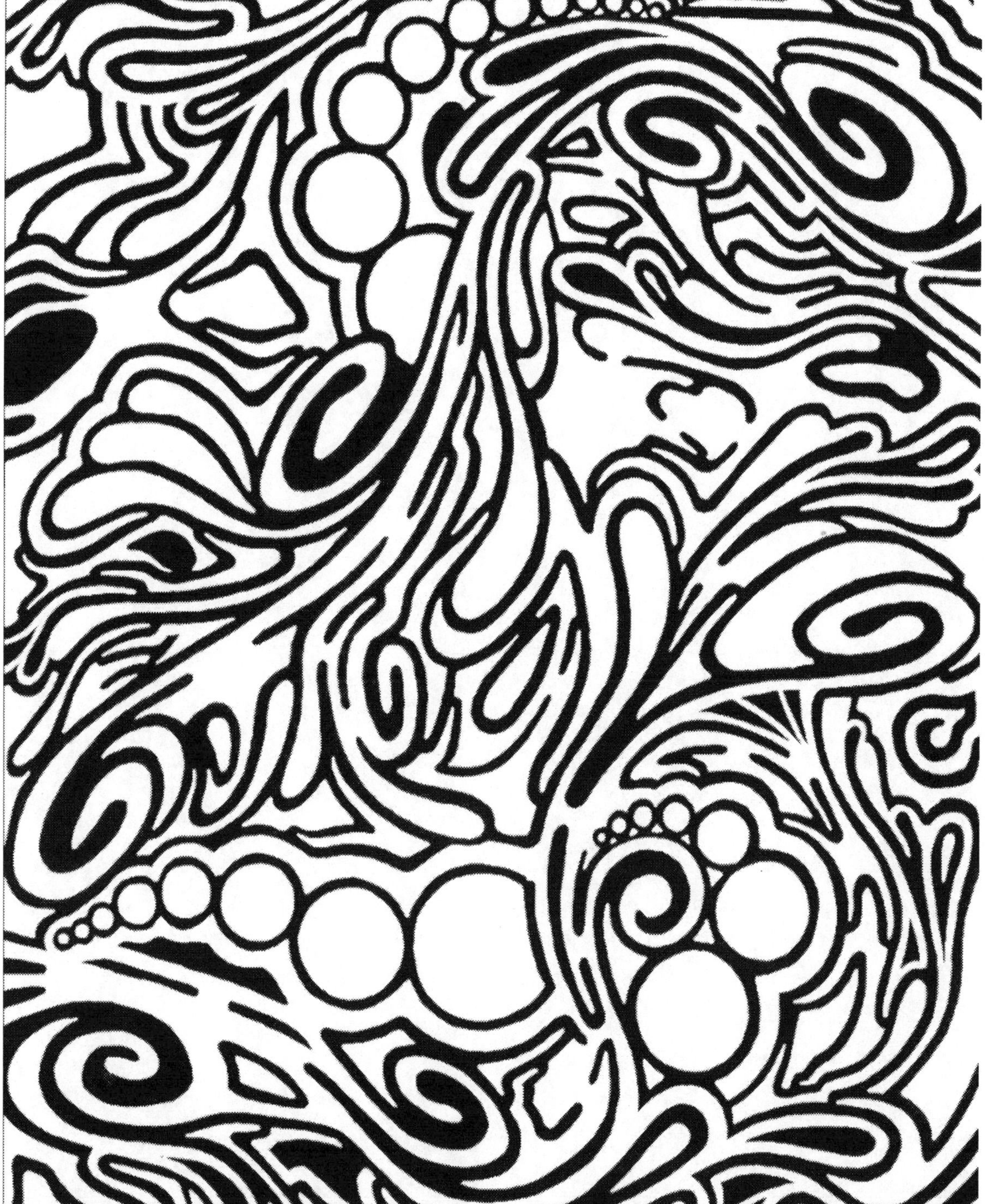

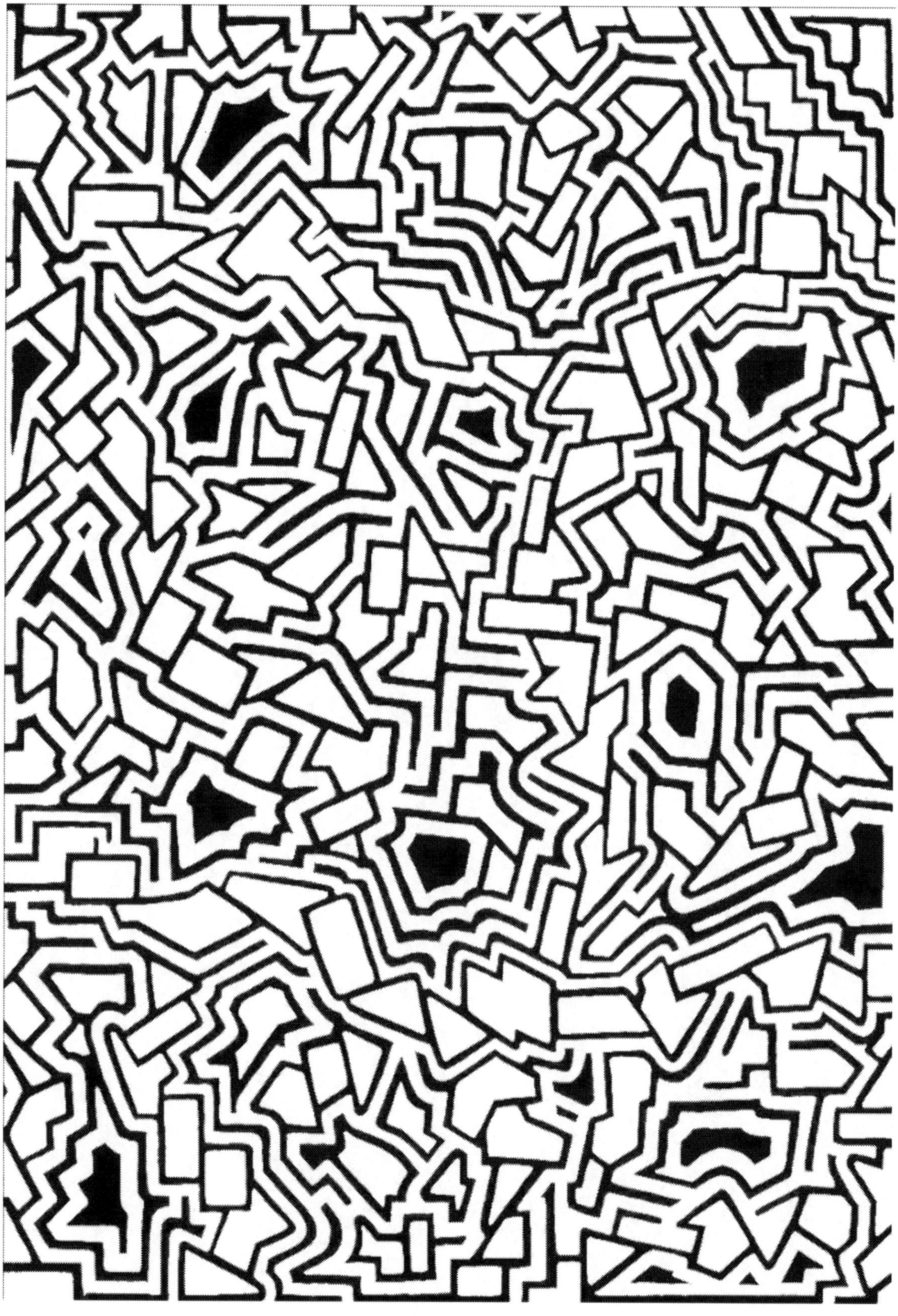

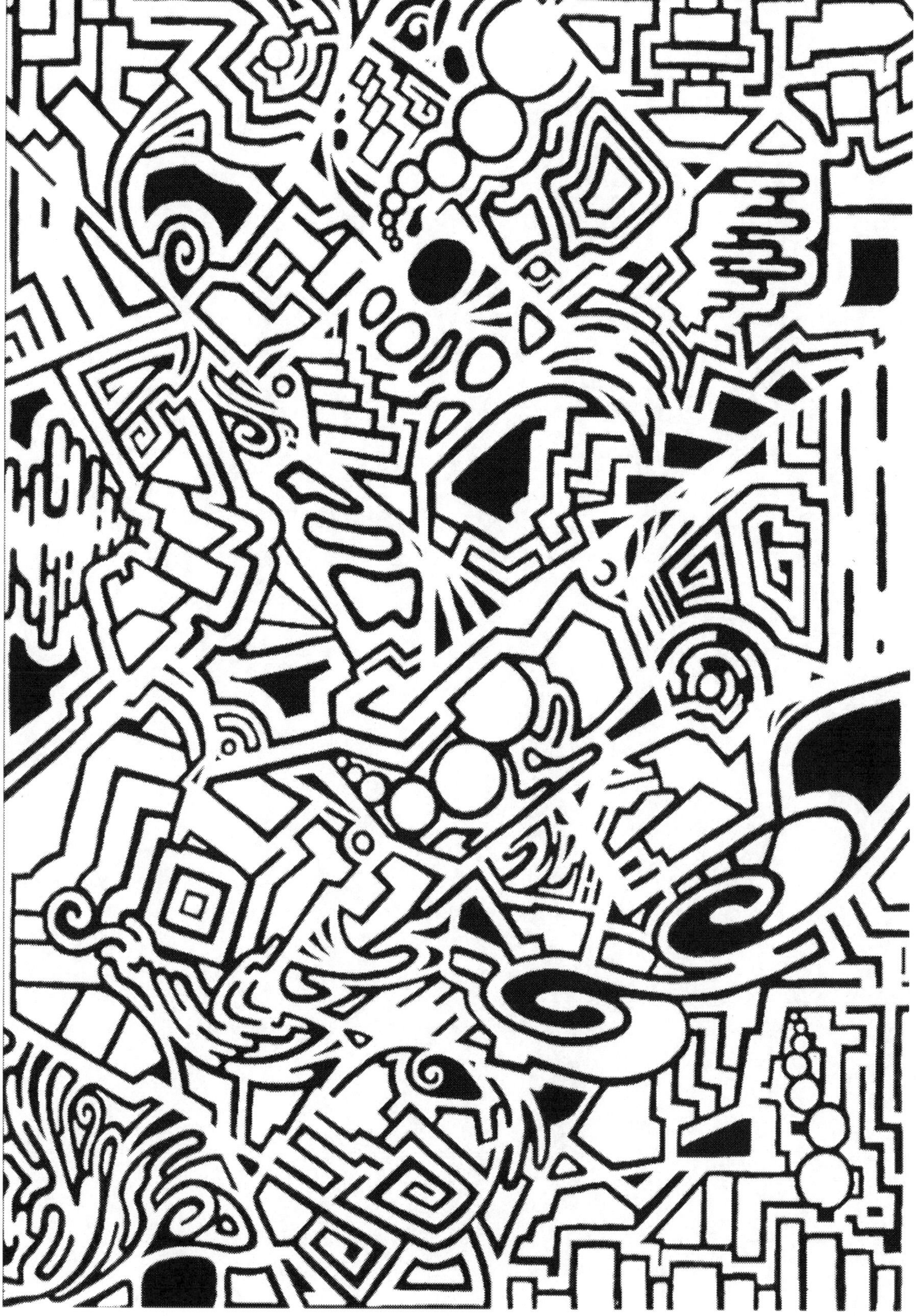

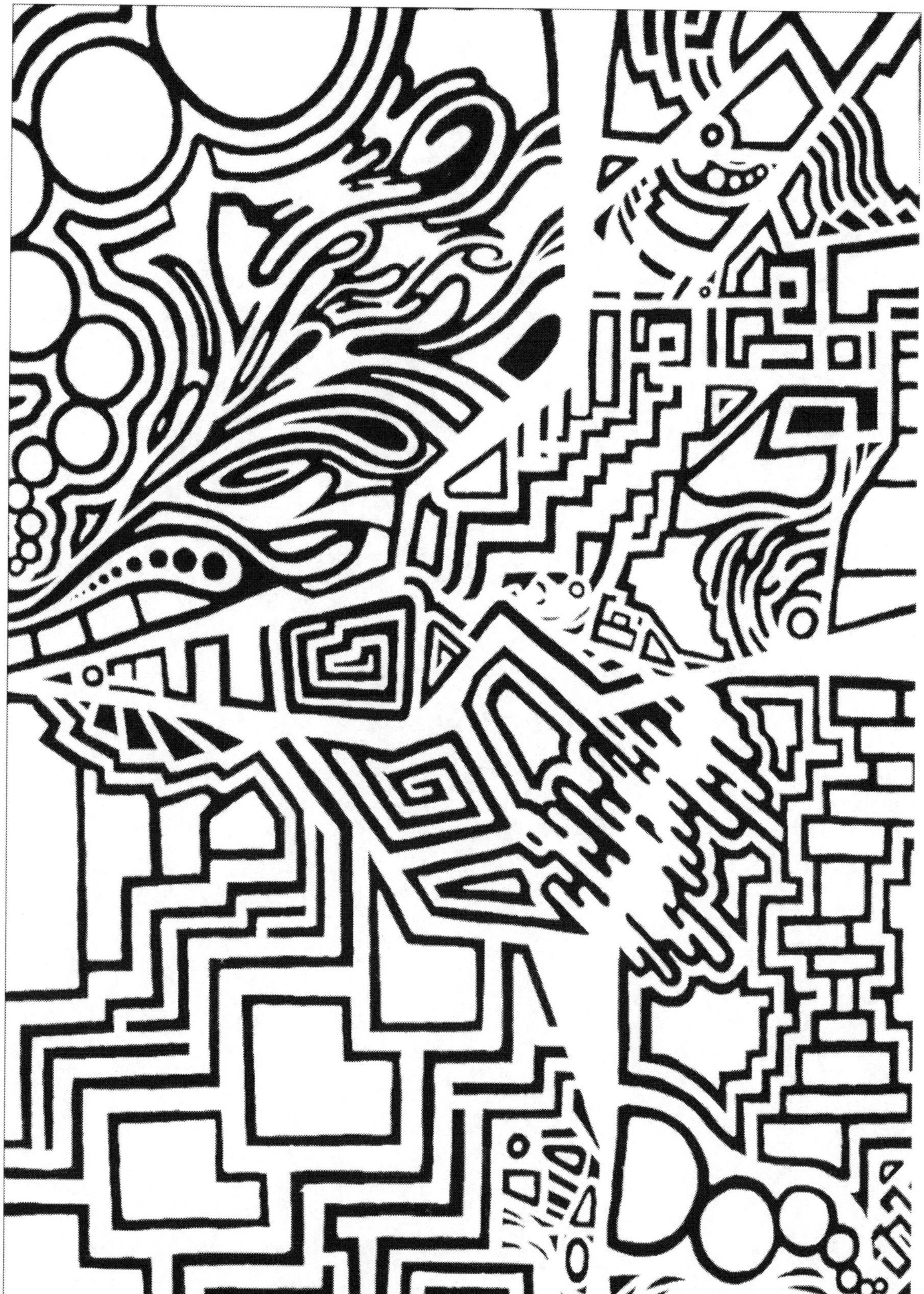

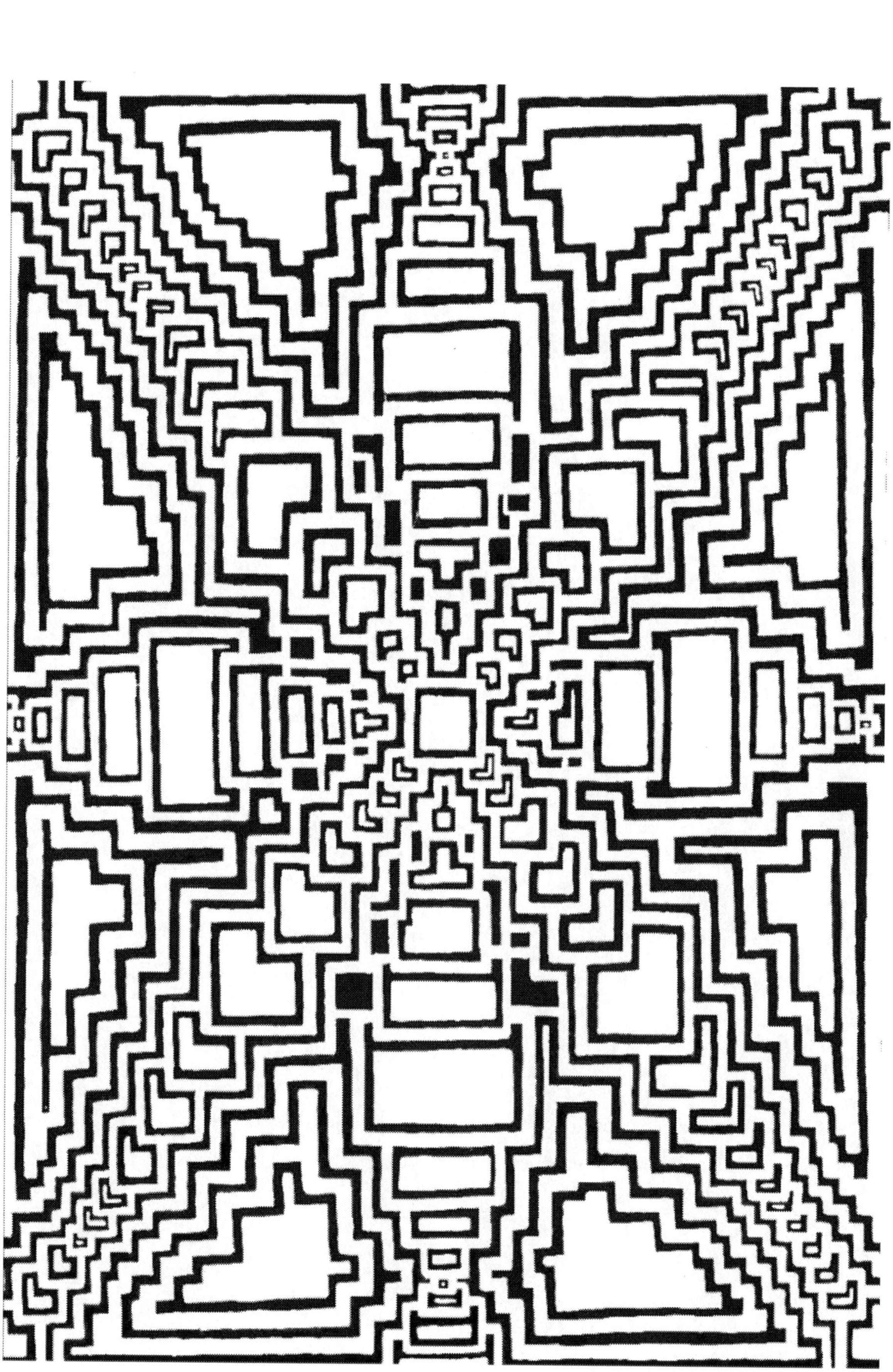

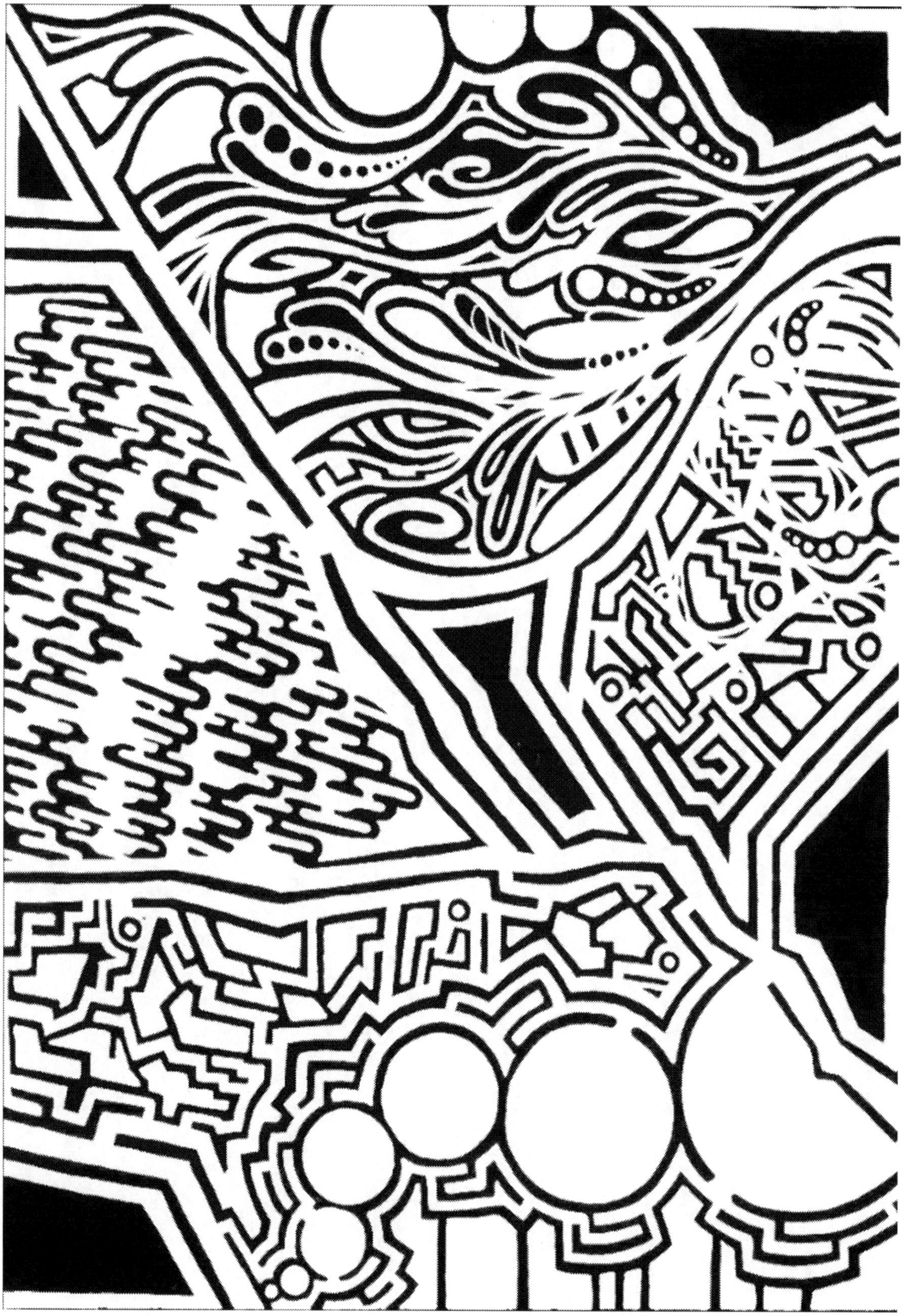

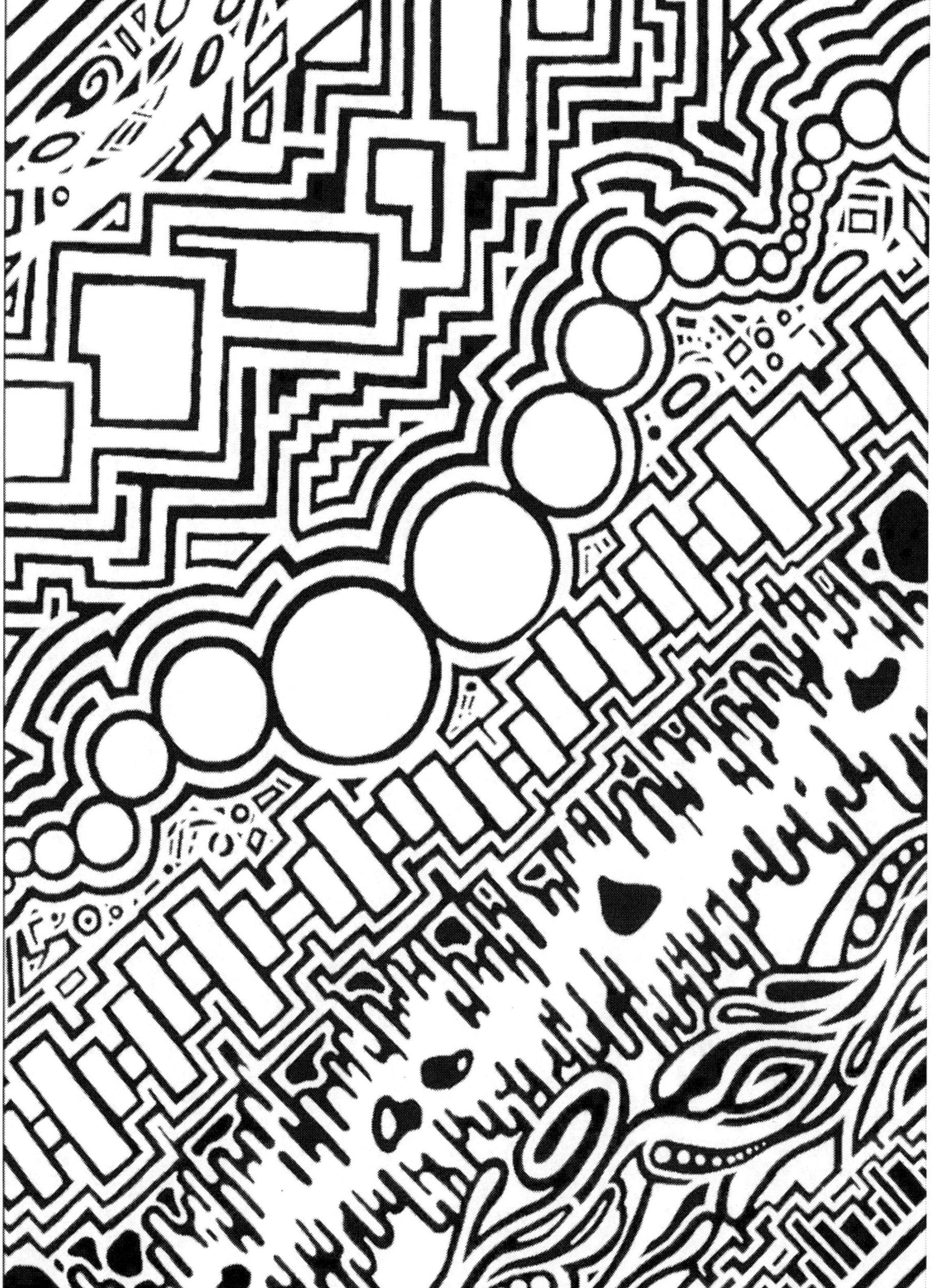

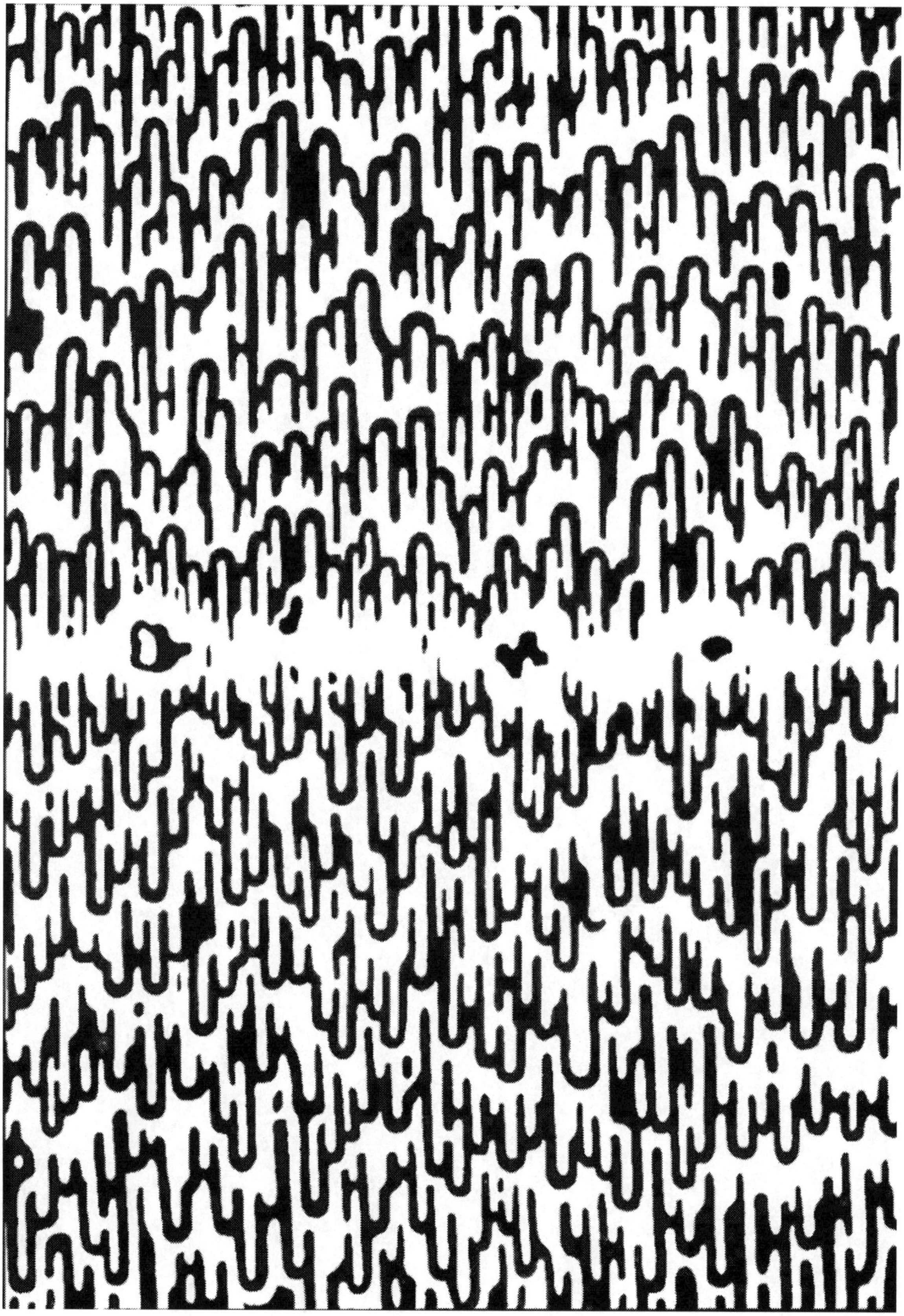

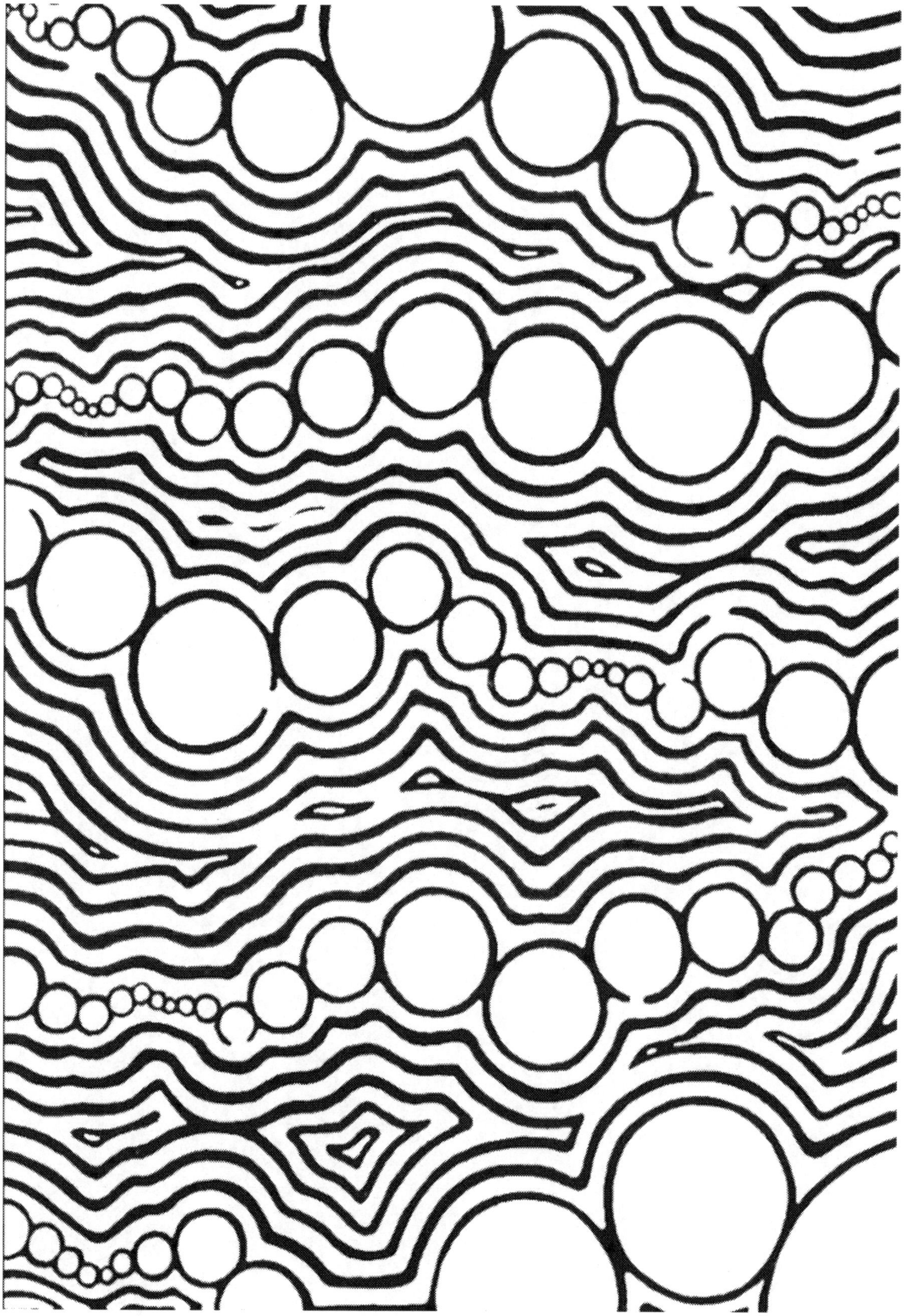

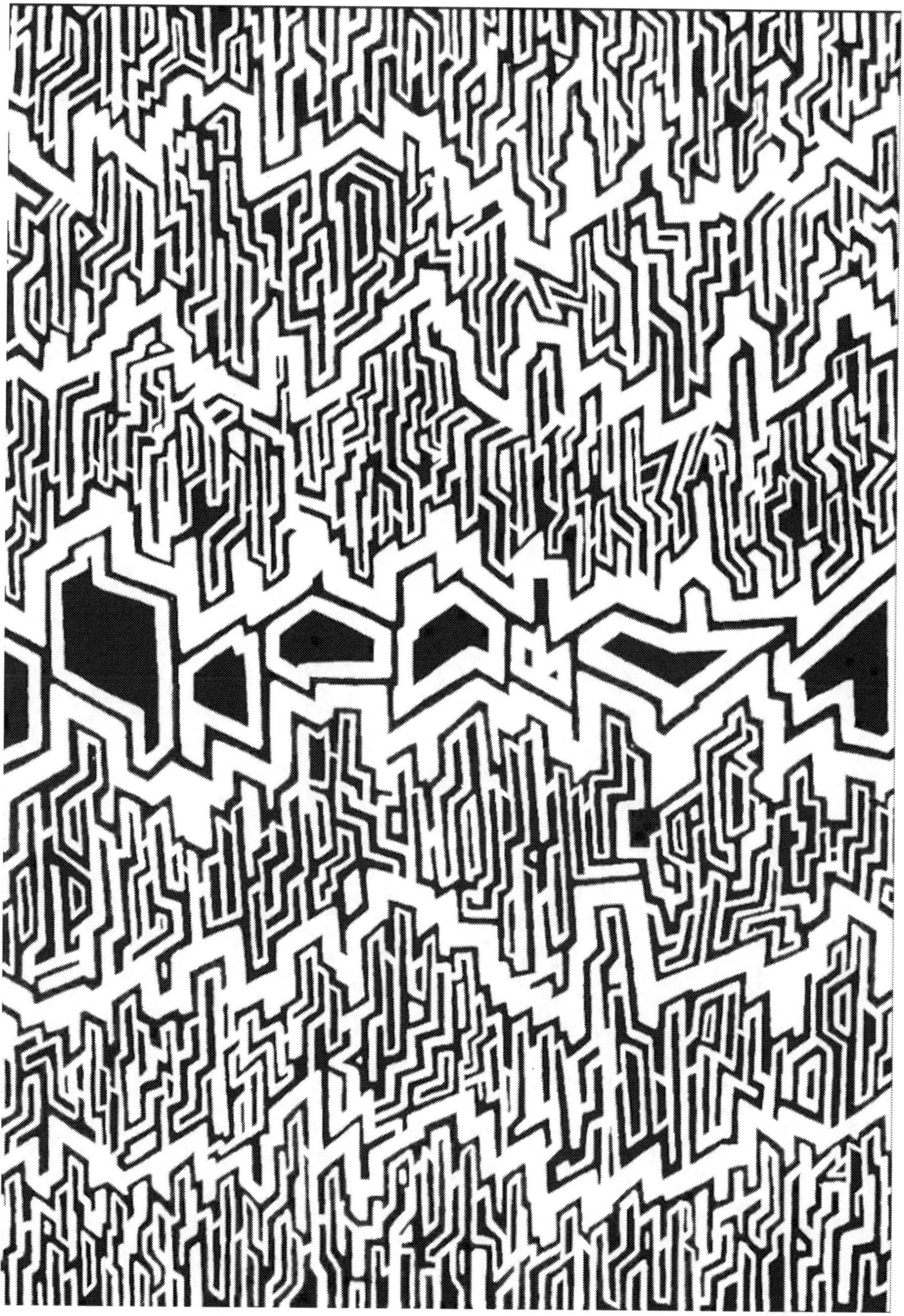

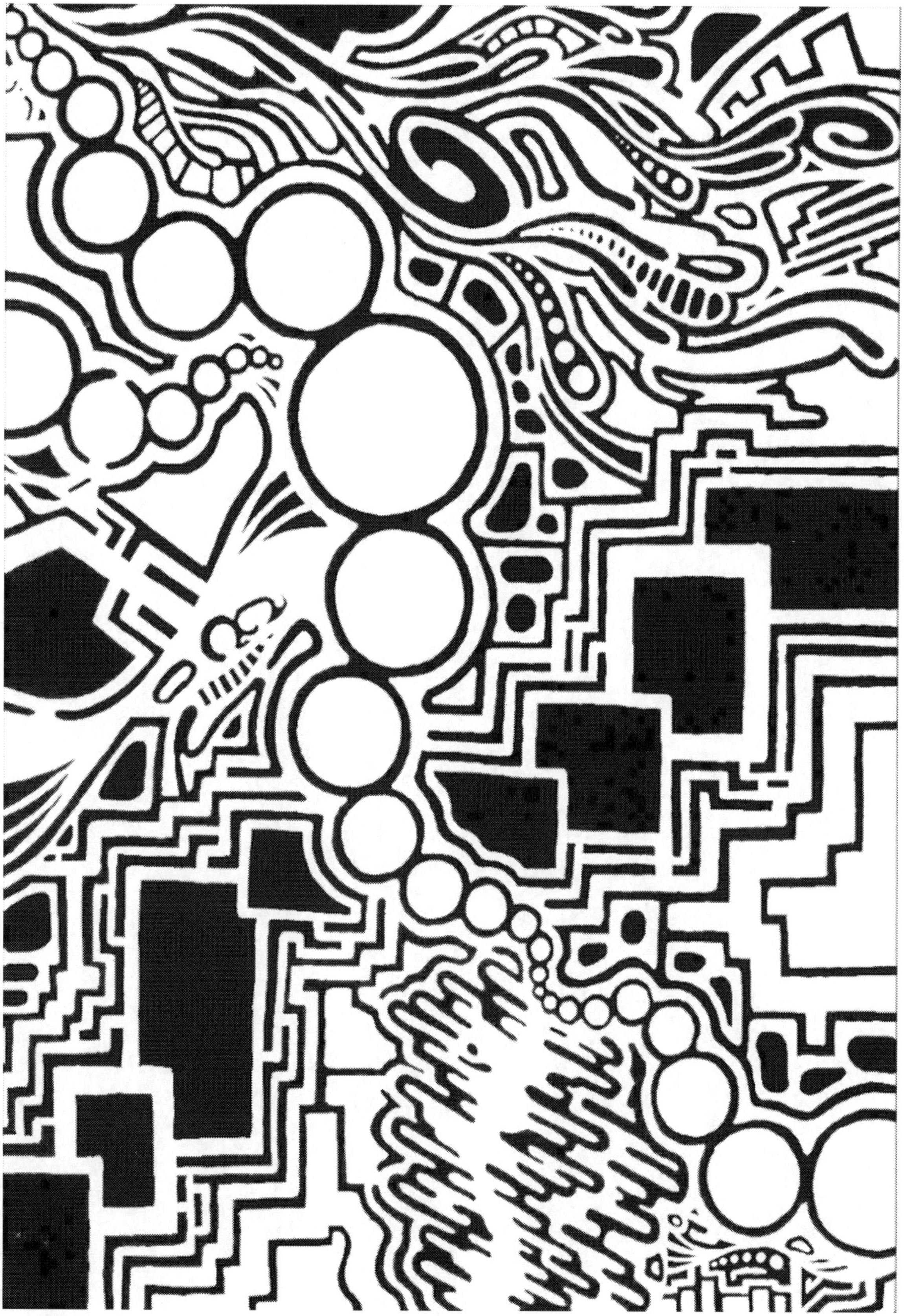

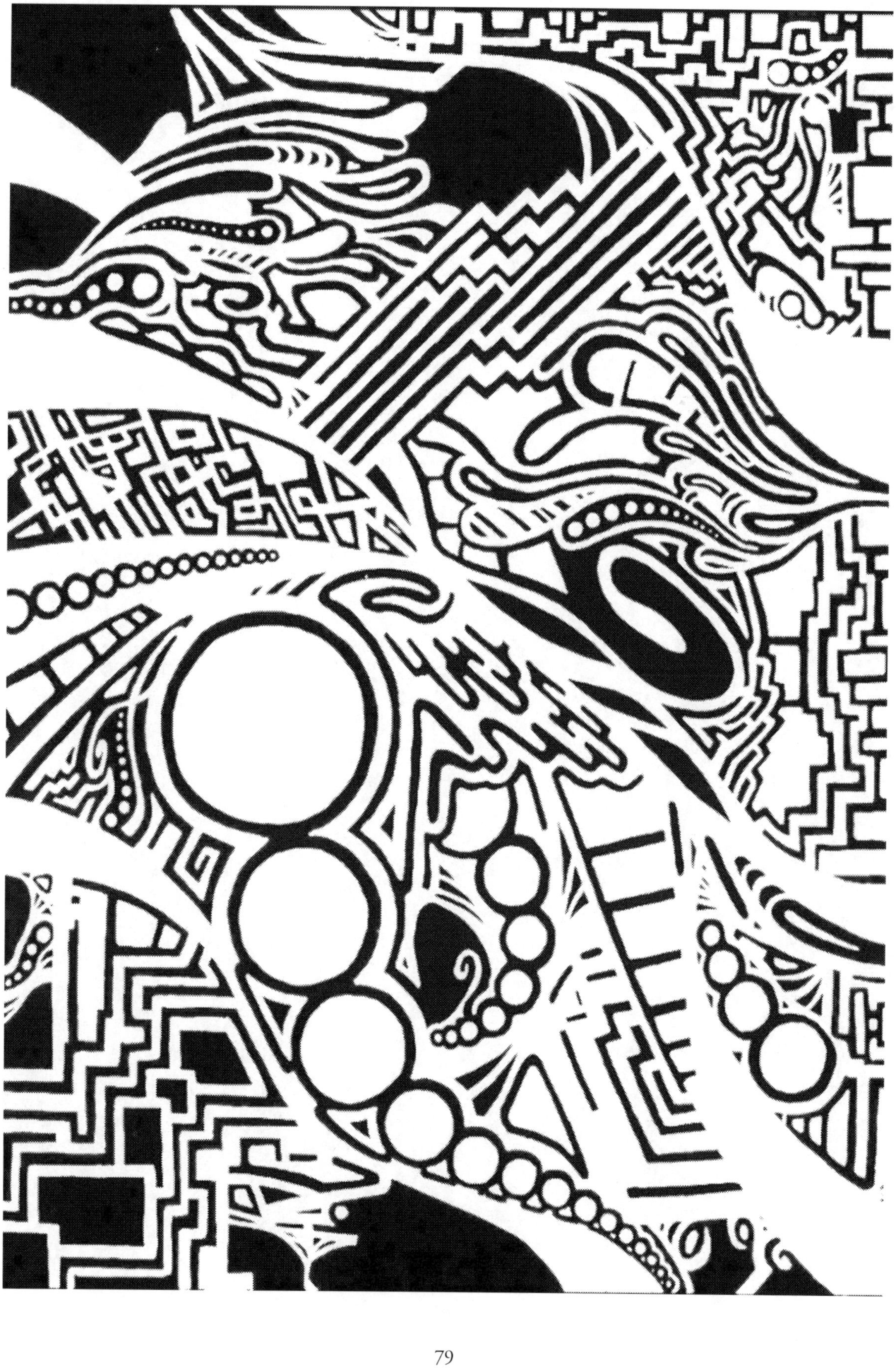

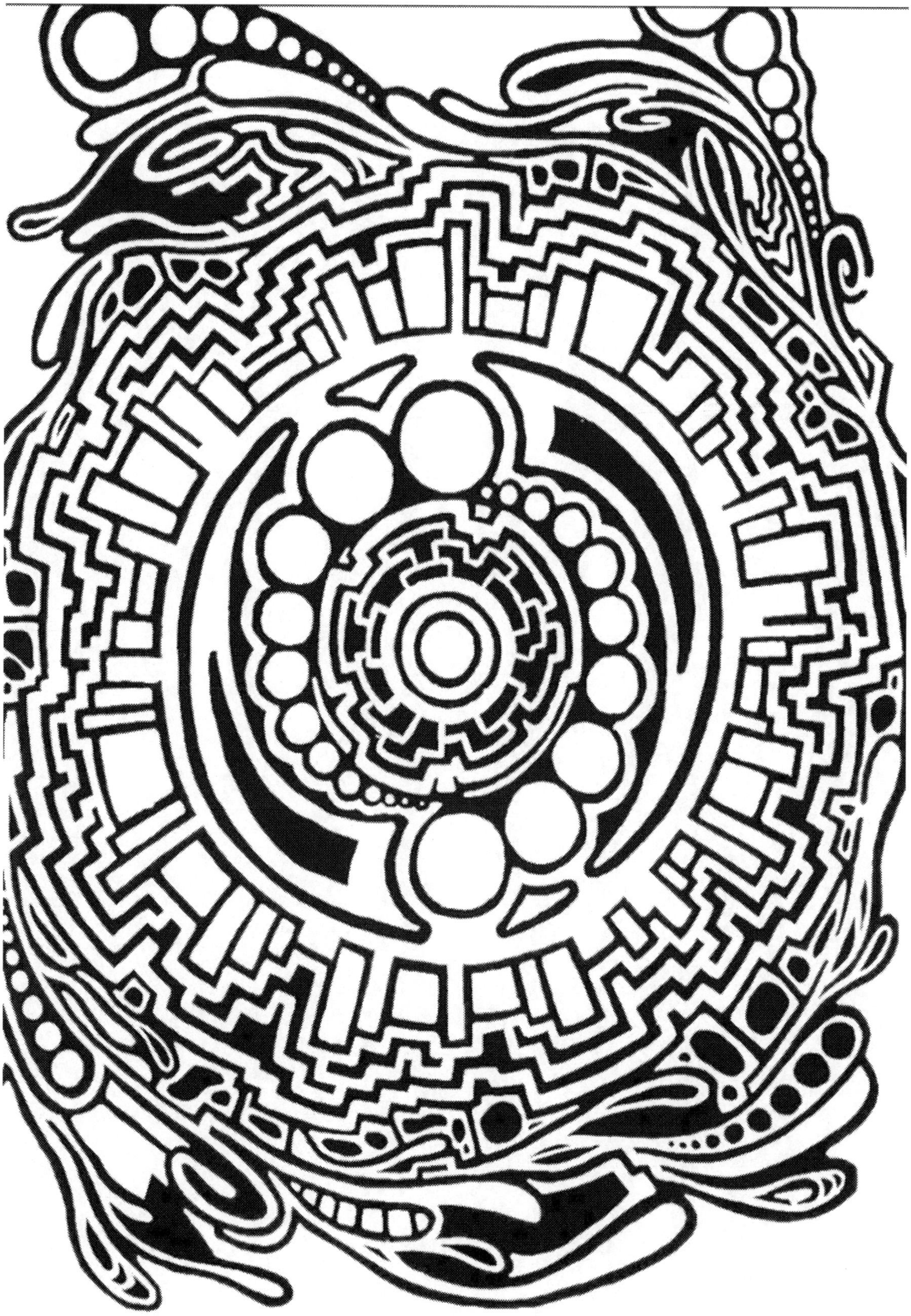

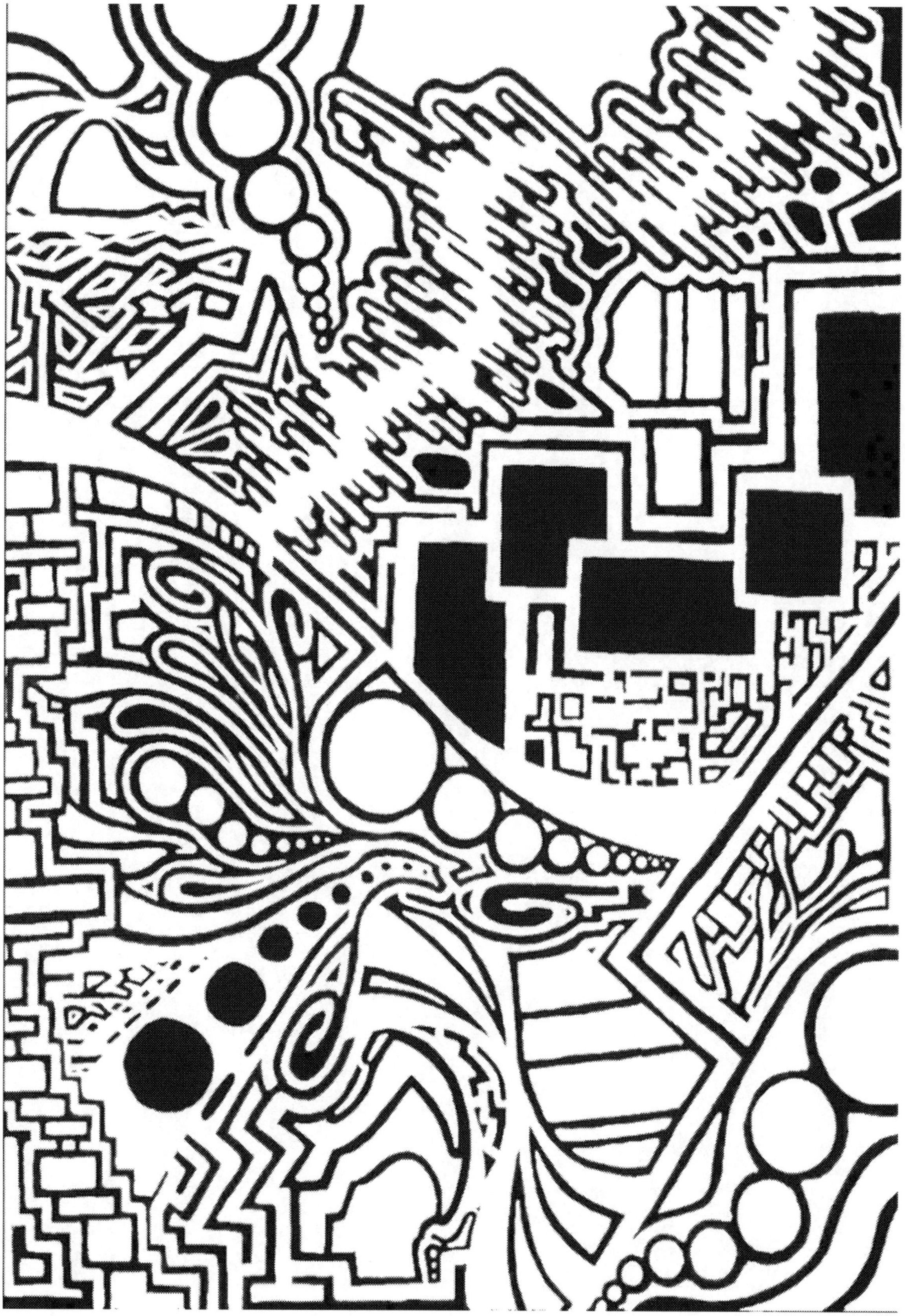

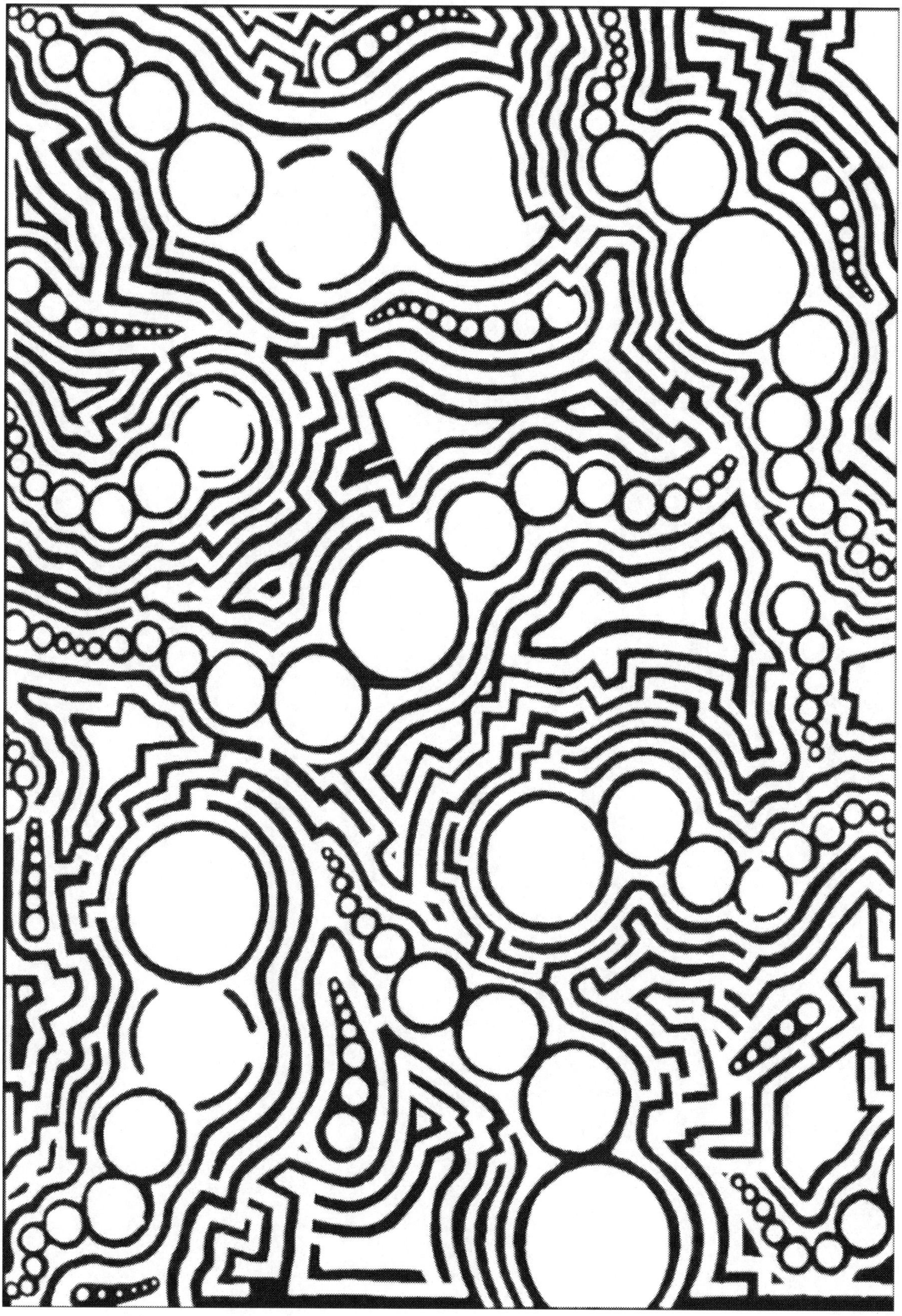

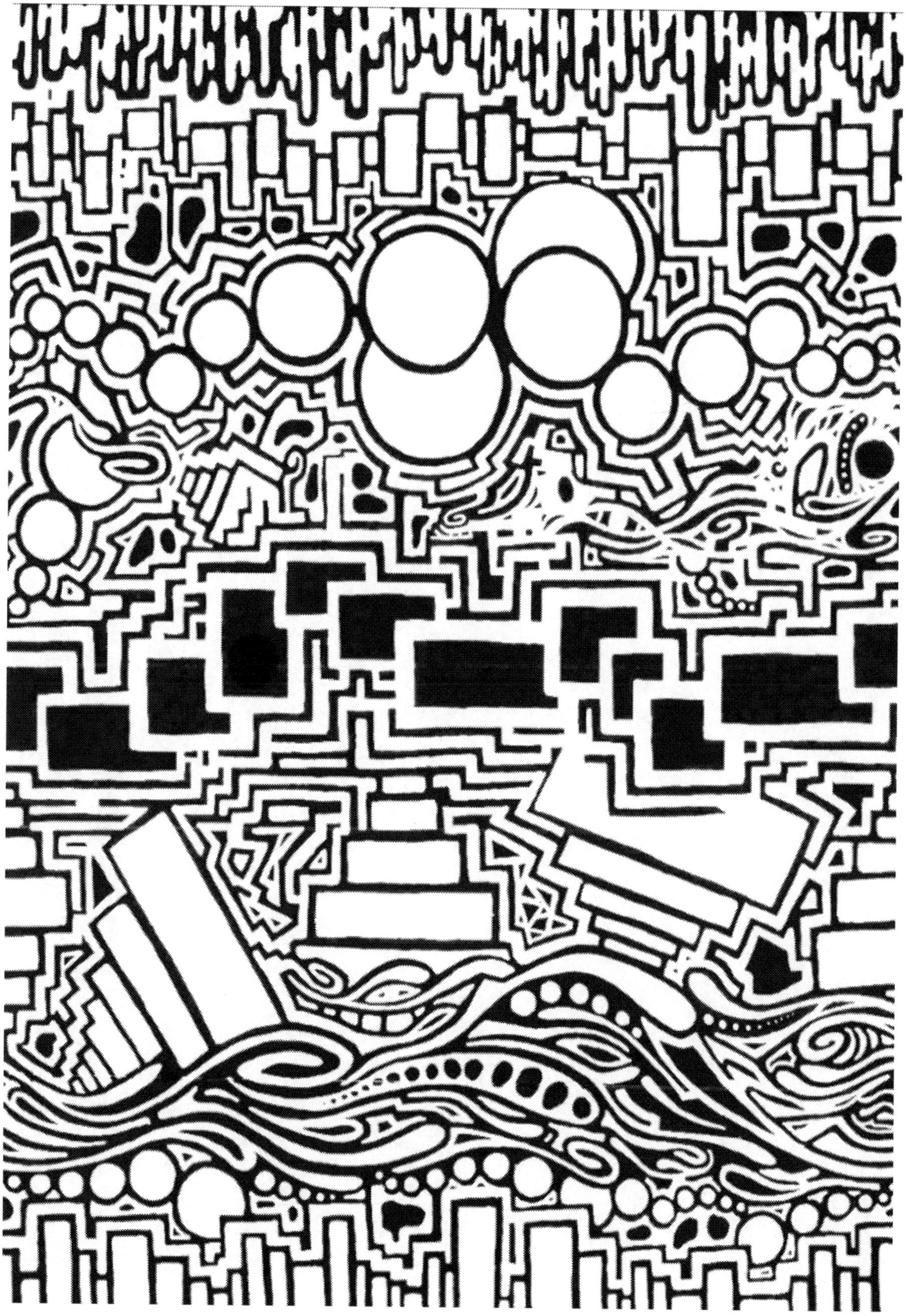

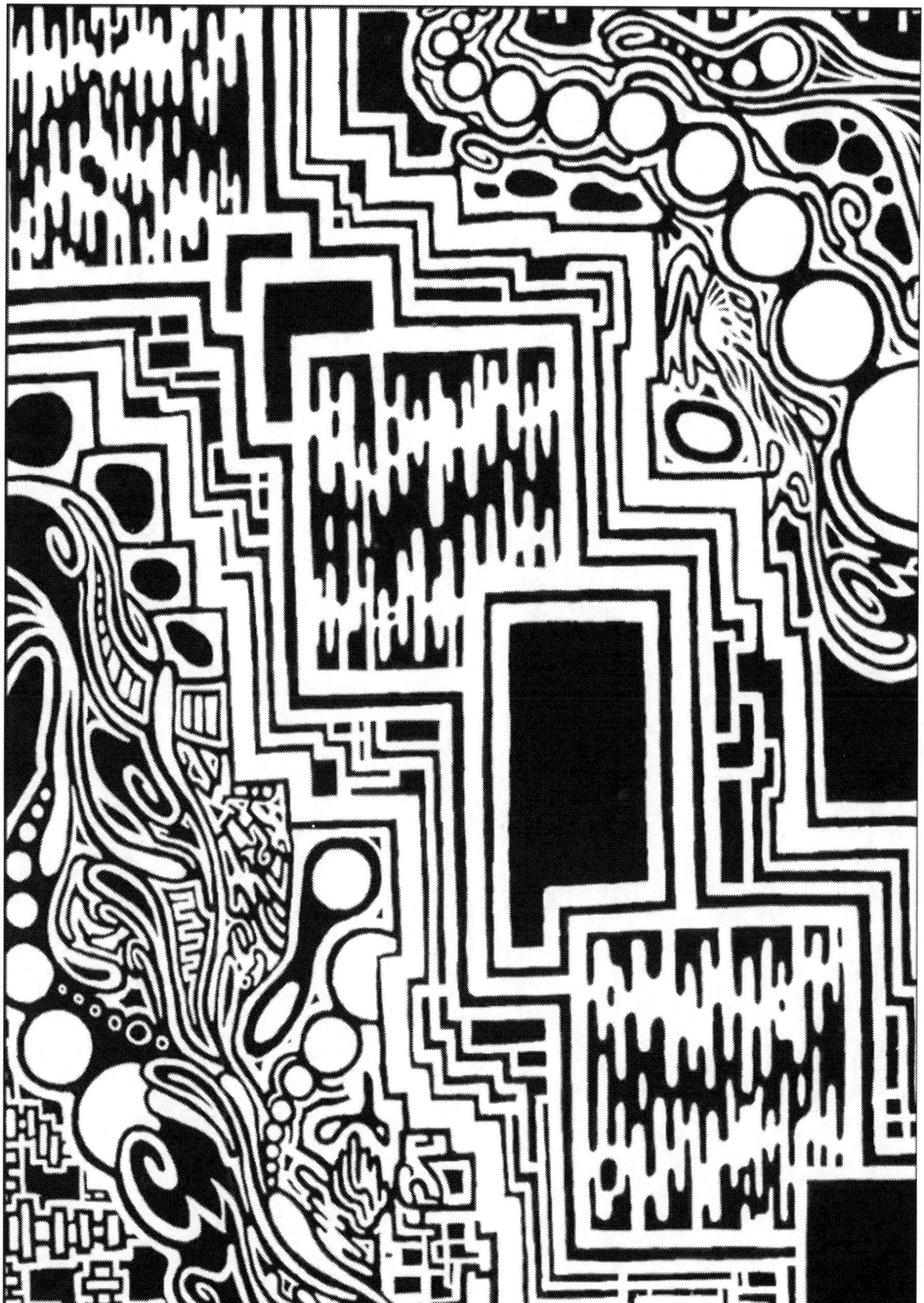

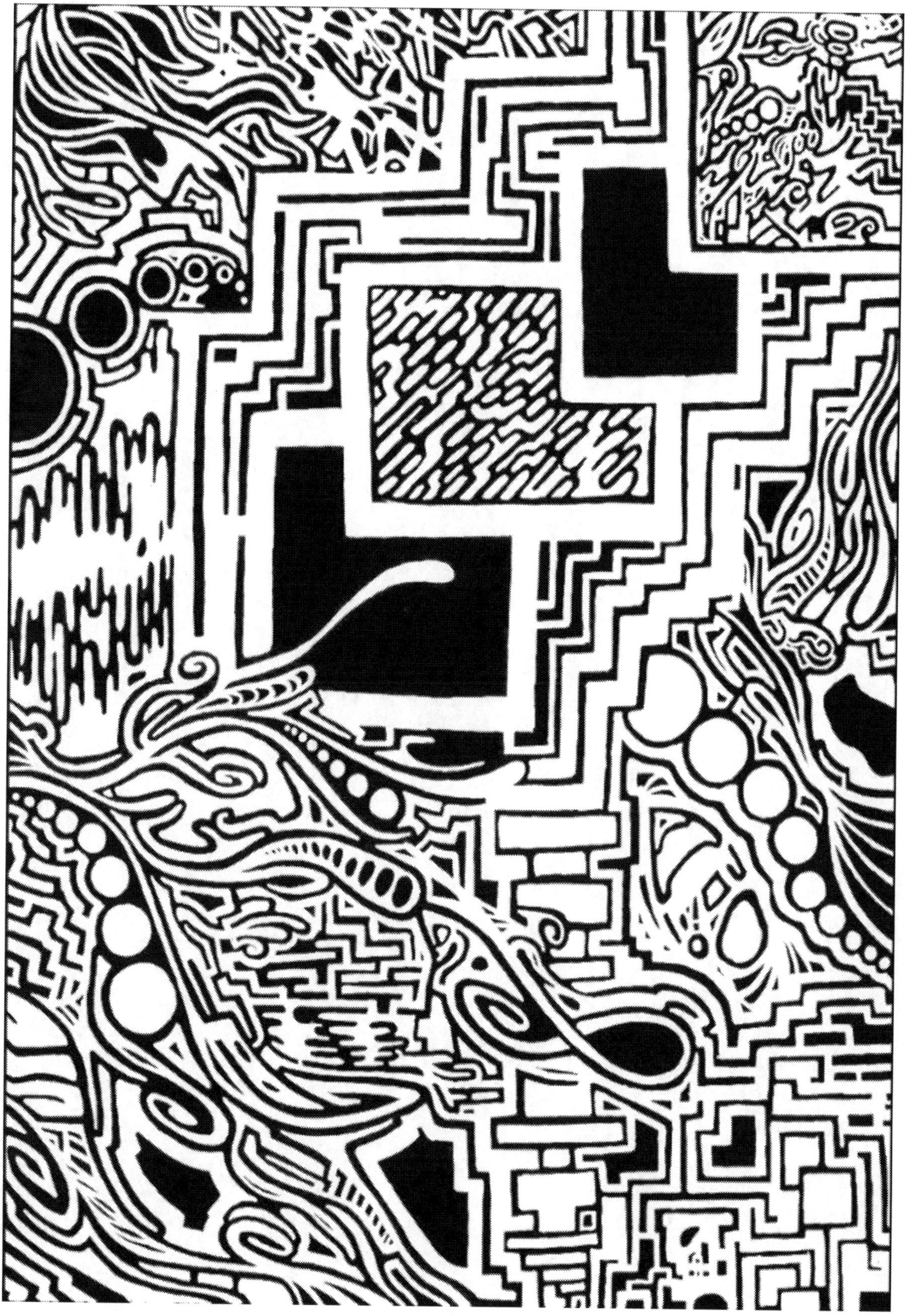

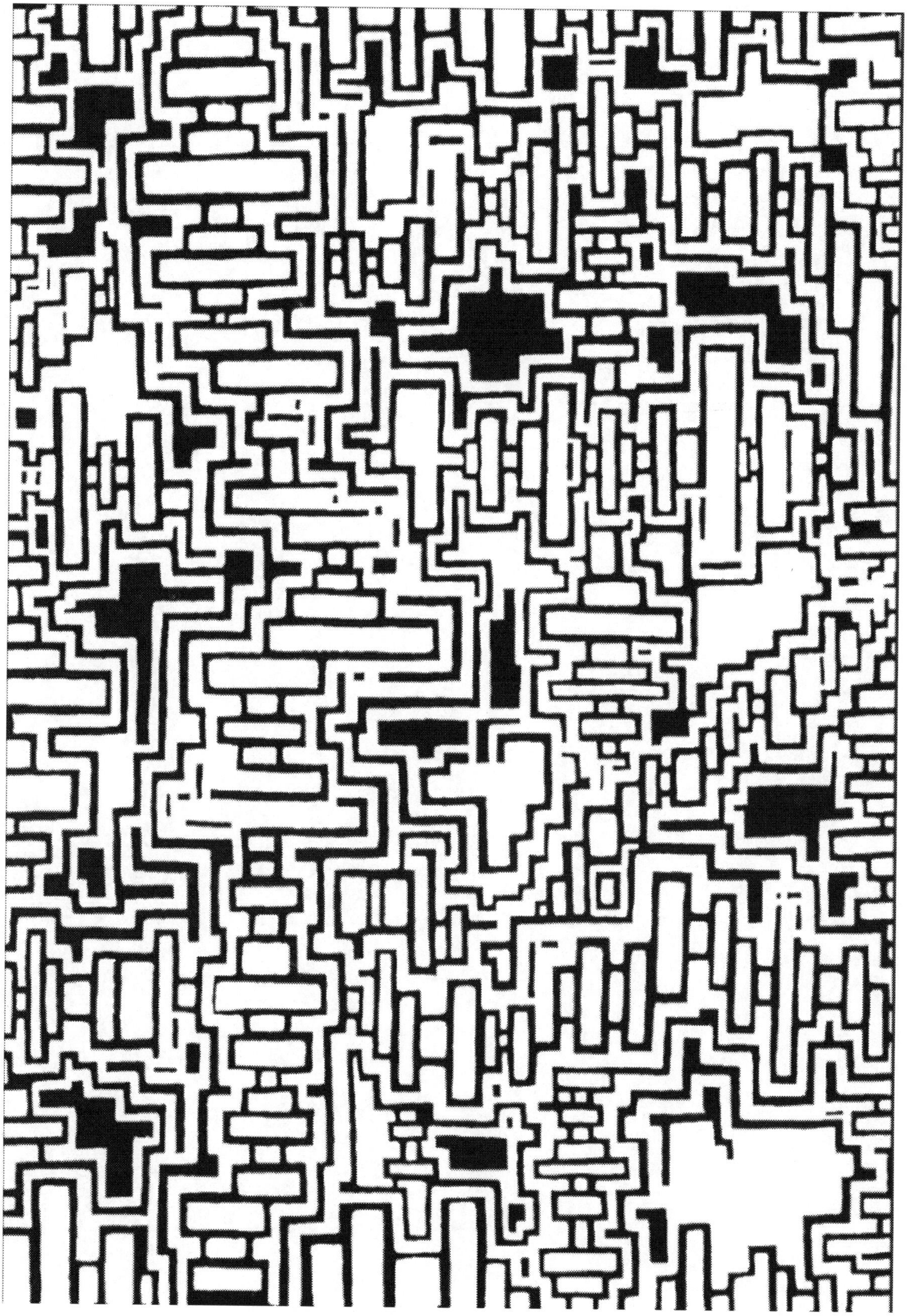

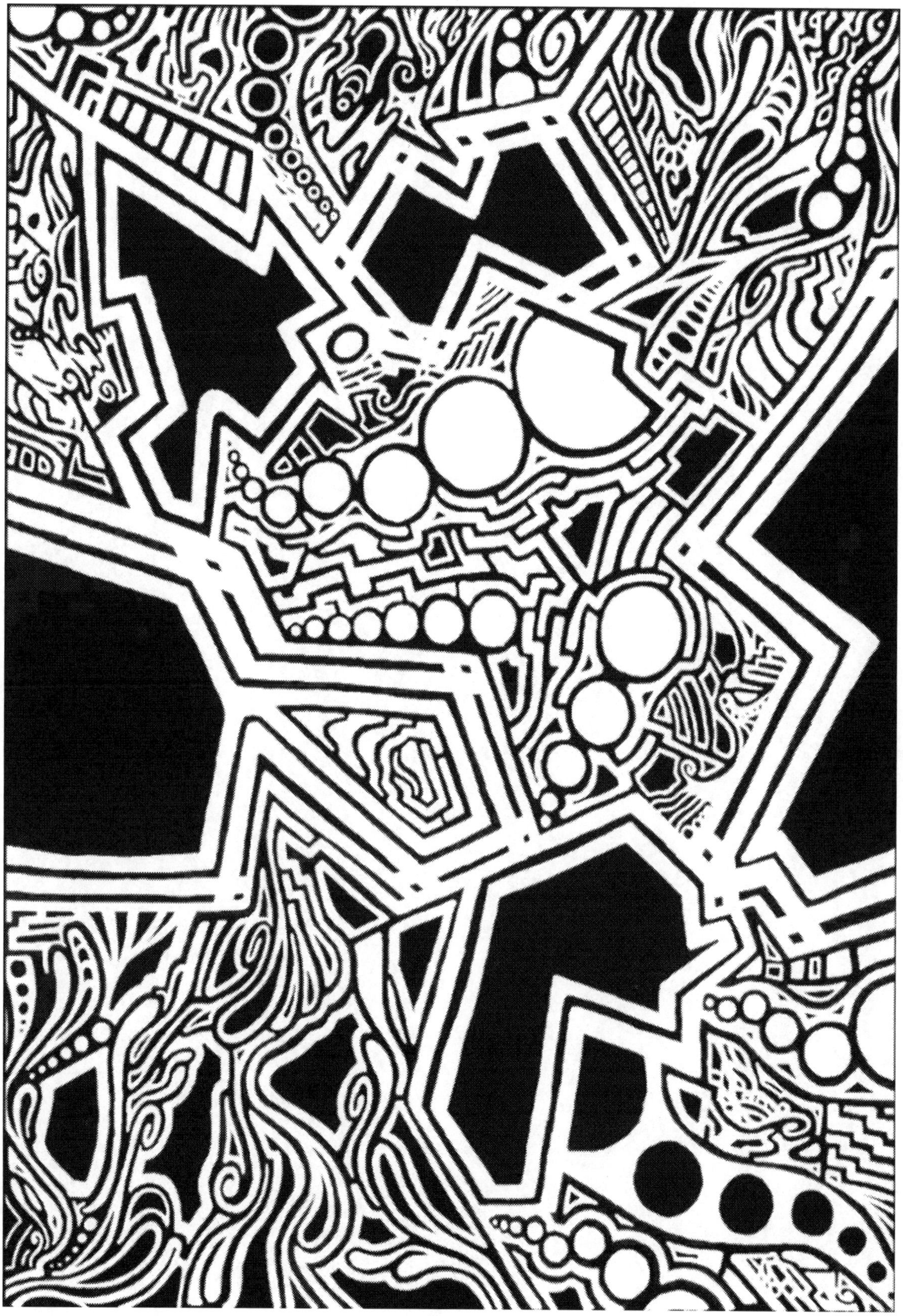

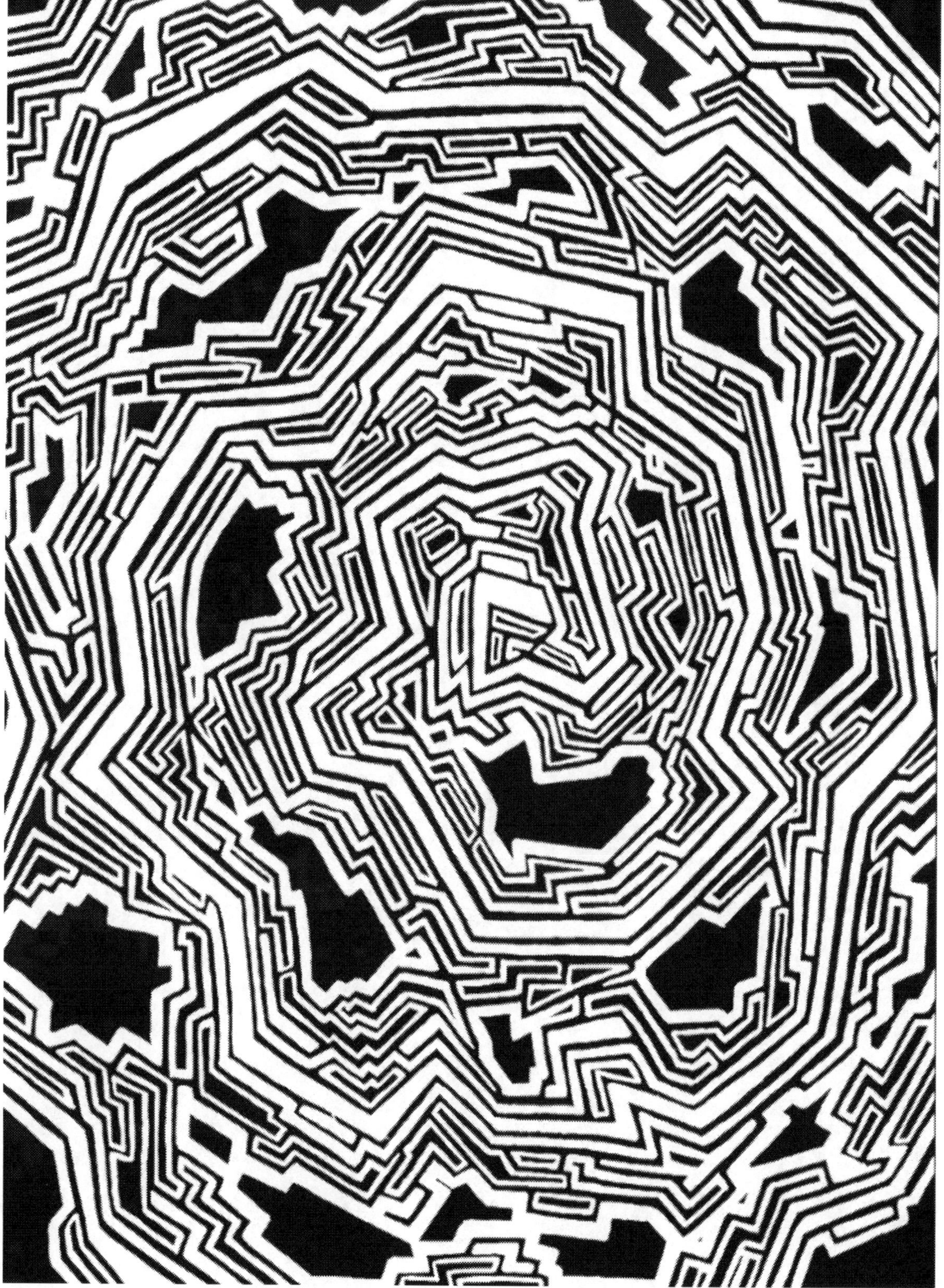

Printed in the United States
by Baker & Taylor Publisher Services